I come from a single parent family. I lived with my mum and my nan and grandad to begin with in Wickford in Essex until I was three years old, then it was just me and my mum who moved together to Basildon.

I was brought up well. I was a good kid: well-behaved, polite and very respectful to my elders. I knew the rules and I abided by them. But somehow…

From a very young age I got into a life of crime, violence and drugs which spiralled out of control very quickly. I completely abused my brain which has now left me with severe mental issues. I suffer with acute transient psychotic disorder, paranoid schizophrenia, OCD, and severe anxiety disorder which makes my life very difficult every single day, from the lasting effects of the life I once lived. By the time that I finish writing this story and it is through the publishing process, I hope to be in a different place in my life and in my head. Let's see if I can make it.

If you have bought this book then I would like to thank you for helping me turn my life around. My aim is to make enough money to not just change mine and my family's life but to help others that are in the position that I once was at a young age, and stop them from suffering mentally in years to come just as I am as I begin this story. A life of violence, crime and drugs will follow you all your life unless you get out before you get too deep. I got too deep and now I suffer for it! But will I forever? or can I turn it around and find peace and return to the respectful person that I was brought up to be at such a young age?

Even a good kid can turn bad!

I would like to dedicate this book to my mother, Mrs Wendy Alicia Buckley Bell who has stuck with me through a life of hell and always seen the good in me even when I turned so bad! Without this woman in my life by my side I truly believe I wouldn't even be here: I would be dead! When I had suicidal thoughts, you were there, and when I was gonna get killed and my murder was planned, you were there. When I was clinically dead at the scene, you were there.

So, thank you mum!

S L Slaven

LOVE OR MONEY

THE DARK SIDE OF ESSEX

AUSTIN MACAULEY PUBLISHERS™

LONDON • CAMBRIDGE • NEW YORK • SHARJAH

A CIP catalogue record for this title is available from the British Library.

ISBN 9781528981255 (Paperback)
ISBN9781528981262 (ePub e-book)

www.austinmacauley.com

First Published 2022
Austin Macauley Publishers Ltd®
1 Canada Square
Canary Wharf
London
E14 5AA

As I'm starting this book, it's the first book I have ever tried to write so my English may not be great but I am just going to say it how I think it, and exactly how it has been to be me.

It's late, it's close to midnight and I'm smoking a strong skunk joint (It's called 'Bruce Banner' incredible hulk strain), it's a new plant. I've also got a bit of 'blue cheese', it's another strain of extra strong weed. I am also addicted to prescription drugs like pregabalin, escitalopram, mirtazapine, diazepam and morphine. I also use cocaine at the weekends but my aim is to be clean by the time I come to the end of this story so stick with me to find out if I can do it. I also need a drug called 'olanzapine', which is 'apparently' the new day equivalent of the same drug that turned Ronnie Kray into a fucking cabbage to calm him down in Broadmoor.

I am chilled to an extent but I am wondering if I'm going to get petrol-bombed tonight, or if my door is going to get kicked in by travellers for turning over a cocaine dealer, which for once (this time) was not true. Well… not entirely! He extorted money from me with the threat of gipsy's kicking my door off to hurt my kids for mossssnths, and it is still going on as I begin to write this book. But let me tell you something, I'm moving house in three days' time, and THEN, this fella is going to feel the full force of my wrath! I will bide my time!

Payback is a bitch and karma is a motherfucker! And you know what? I can be a nasty bastard too! The part traveller in me will NEVER let that go, the threat to my child!! I am about to write a crazy fucked up story that you would not believe about somebody's life... Mine... I'm not going to give you an autobiography as such, no dates or times of events in my life. I am just going to tell you my true story, roughly, how it happened. Even writing this book is going to take me to some dark places in my mind and in turn probably affect me temporarily in other ways!)

So why am I writing this story? That I cannot answer; it's just something I feel like I have to do. Is it about the money? As you will see, probably not, as I could have made millions in other ways throughout my life. There is a lot of information in this story that could get me in a whole world of trouble with the wrong kind of people and bring me serious drama, but it's those very people I still kind of have a strange kind of love for and certainly want to thank for helping to turn me into the man with a story I am today!

As I write this story I'm living in a council flat in, let's just say, a famous part of Essex and for reasons that will become obvious (and some that won't) later, I'd rather keep to myself as I am moving but I'm not going far. I'm 34 years old and I'm still putting up with this shit and spending my life looking over my shoulder. I just hope and pray that by the end of this story it's calmed down a bit.

Before I start let me give you a little insight into how my brain works nowadays, after all the drug abuse from a young age. First of all, if I am watching TV, I MUST have the volume on number 33 as I am 34 and if I have it on 34, it means I will die at this age (34) and if I have it any higher then that is the age I will die. So if I do need to hear something a bit louder I have to turn it right up to above 80 so I don't die young and do reach the age of 80. Huh, this is nothing. The struggles in my head every day all day are a task in itself to deal with. Anyway, moving on, I have 13 steps up to my flat and at certain times if something bad enters my head I MUST take the steps two at a time so that it equals seven when I get to the top, otherwise, the bad thought (usually death-related) I'm having at that precise moment will come true and happen to me.

Also, when a bad thought or a paranoid thought enters my head in the middle of the day at any random time, I have to do certain body movements four times every single time. It's a movement I cannot tell anybody about and also nobody can see me do this movement otherwise it all cancels out in my head and my protection is gone (this has never happened). It's almost what you would call a 'tik'. I can't even see myself in a shadow or a reflection of any kind as I do this body movement four times to stop the bad things (like death) from happening to me. Now, this happens, I would say about 40 to 50 times a day, every single day of my life and it makes everyday life difficult, to say the least. I think a lot of it, apart from my paranoid schizophrenia, acute transient psychotic disorder and anxiety disorders is my past haunting me as I spend my life still looking over my shoulder. There are people who would like to see me dead and buried in the ground and I would guess there's a few coppers that would love to nick me and see me behind bars for good, that's for sure!

Now for a little insight into how I was brought up and the family I came from.

As a baby, I lived with my mum and my nan and granddad, who both worked their fingers to the bone but were well off for it until the age of three. Then my mum and I moved into a council place in Basildon, Essex. I still spent every single weekend with my grandparents during my childhood years. My mother spent this time (every single weekend) getting through about four bottles of vodka and hitting 'time' which was nightclub in Basildon. She liked a good drink and the company of men. I hated this!

At the start though, my mother and I had nothing at all in the way of furniture to begin with; just a small table and two beach type deckchairs and a cassette playing radio and I think, a black and white portable TV with a coat hanger for an aerial and two trays to eat our dinner from our laps. I must say, my mum did her best and we had a lot of support from my grandparents over the years but I would never let my mum work. One reason was because I was a mummy's boy and very clingy and the other reason was the fear of being left at 'the childminder's' where I was being sexually abused which would not surface until I was well into my adult years.

My father was not around which was really hard at times but I'm led to believe that if he had been around things could have been a damn sight harder. My mother denies telling me this but she did tell me that my dad was a monster, or maybe I overheard it, as one day my mum received a letter from Brian. He wrote that once he was released from prison he would come to get me. She probably didn't mean it in the way that I took it but it caused me to have a recurring nightmare for years where a giant green monster banged on our front door screaming and shouting my name before kicking through the door, shoving my mother on the floor and climbing the stairs to my room where I would be hiding under my bed covers. This monster would then proceed to pick me up under his arm and run out of the house with me, and my mother would be screaming hysterically but helpless against this giant. He would run out of our road and I would wake up at the same part of the nightmare every time, just as the monster reached the end of the road!

I had this nightmare for a couple of years at least once a month and it was always exactly the same! Though I now know it was best for me, it was really hard without a real dad in my life. I always wondered where he was. I would later be bullied for this (not having a father). I was fortunate to be taken on holidays abroad as a child too, whether it was my mum paying or my nan and granddad taking us away. I vividly remember one holiday in particular.

It was a couple of weeks before Christmas and me and my mum were over my nan and granddad's, which was nothing out of the ordinary but the family seemed excited. I was 7 years old, I was told I had an early Christmas present which I must open on that day (I wasn't keen on surprises I got easily embarrassed as a child). I had no idea at all what it could possibly be. A couple of hours passed and I could feel the excitement from the adults in the air, literally. I was handed a small gift; it felt like a little oblong booklet, it was bendy and paper-like. Everyone was gathered around me. As I opened it (with a lot of encouragement as I was a shy boy), I saw the words 'DESTINATION', 'FLIGHT NUMBER' and 'FLORIDA'.

I said, "Is this what I think it is?"

"Oh my god, I'm going to Disney World in America," and for Christmas!!! It was to be a three-week trip of a lifetime without a doubt. I broke down crying with overwhelming happiness and joy. We were going as a whole family, me, my mum, my nan and my granddad. I don't know what airport it was when I caught my first glimpse out of a window, but I never forgot that familiar sight of a sea of yellow taxi cabs. It was surreal, at the time I would have simply described it as an 'amazing sight'. I mean, people buy framed pictures nowadays of that sort of thing to hang on their walls at home.

What you see in the Christmas films is exactly how it really is! Every single house and its neighbour had an expensive and extravagant light display from moving Santas and reindeer to 10ft snowmen lit up and waving whilst every other house on each street would play Christmas music for a period of the evening. The Americans certainly know how to celebrate the festive season and make it magical for not just the kids but for everybody. We visited all the major theme parks and attractions and also frequented the local American diners of an evening, this really was the trip of a lifetime, A trip that I would love to give to my children one day but I would need to stop taking drugs first!

Thank you to my now passed grandad, Mr Bernie Bell. (The only man I ever looked up to, a true gentleman and always my dream maker). The man always made sure I got whatever I really wanted for birthdays and Christmas, as a big surprise I suppose to make up for not having a father. He was my father figure for sure, and a great role model who I would unfortunately stray from being alike. My mum tells me she left my real dad when I was a few months old for our safety

12

as he was violent and very mentally ill man with a vicious temper, kind of like me.

Colin (my stepdad) was in my life from a very young age, from around a year old, then my mum left him for cheating on her on more than one occasion. My mum had quite a few boyfriends, sometimes more than one at a time; she was a player! I used to go to bed petrified of my mum and her fella going to bed because my mother was, let's just say, 'loud in the bedroom'; I hated it. I didn't get it. I didn't really know what was going on but my mum was definitely addicted to sex, would I later follow suit? I, even out of my pocket money, bought a Walkman so that I could go to bed each night listening to it to drown out the noise, but sometimes my mum was so loud that I would still hear her and it would make me cry myself to sleep.

Some days my mother used to send me outside to play with the other kids but then her bedroom curtains would close and then there would be no answer at the door for over an hour or two, If I listened at the door I could clearly hear what was going on.

Then eventually, my mum got married to a fella called Wallace Fisher (which is where my name 'Fisher' stuck from). It only lasted a couple of years, and Wallace got caught cheating too, so my mum divorced him. I changed my name back to my biological father's name but 'Fisher' had stuck. A few more boyfriends passed and it wasn't long until Colin was back on the scene. He has looked after my mum well ever since and they are still together. I've always known I had a dad out there but Colin has been my dad for as long as I can remember. I remember my mum taking me to a wimpy restaurant in Basildon town centre and saying to me that as I was old enough to read the newspaper, I should know my biological father was in the news for kidnap and torture, and if I remember right, he got a few years for it.

For a long time I heard stories from various people. I was told he was not to be fucked with and to put it bluntly, he's off his fucking rocker! I didn't read about it in the papers but later on in life, I heard one of the many versions of this story. Apparently, three blokes went to Brian's house to pay a debt they had with him for drugs. Anyway, Brian must have had a psychotic episode or something because he said that these fellas had robbed his gold from the table, so he locked the blokes in a room and beat them and starved and tortured them until the police found them about a week later in a mess and after all that, the gold that was meant to have been taken from Brian had been put away but as a kid, apart from the monster dreams that occurred because of things that were said, I'd never heard much about Brian, 'my biological father'. What I was hearing was not good even though it excited me if I'm honest.

He was a head doorman and a big figure in the criminal underworld in and around Essex for quite some years just before the 'Essex boys' business with Pat Tate and Tony Tucker really kicked off. I hear that Brian was sort of pushed aside by the firms in Essex because of his mental health. He was a liability in the sense that he was a loose cannon and completely unpredictable with it.

Life at home was strict but actually not bad at all. I had a very good upbringing, that is putting aside all the arguing between my mother and stepdad. I used to sit at the top of the stairs listening and wincing every time the screaming started again or something got smashed up against the wall. I hated him for the continuous cheating on my mum but now that I'm older I realise how hard it was for Colin (my stepdad). He did do all the important things like teaching me how to swim and ride a bike, all those things you need a dad for. He also taught me a trade when I dropped out of school at 14 years old. My mum said I either work or get out as I wasn't at school, so Colin took me to work as a tiler and showed me everything I needed to know. I stuck it out for years but I can't do it anymore due to the fact I have been diagnosed with severe paranoid schizophrenia and acute transient psychotic disorder hence the medication I mentioned at the beginning of this story, all will be explained!!

Through infants and juniors, I was bullied daily, every fuckin' day I can remember, mainly for not having a dad. I was called a 'bastard' every time I was getting beaten up and kicked the shit out of as I laid on the floor taking the blows dealt by crowds of little shits. One day I remember running all the way home to my mum because I was being beaten up and again being called a bastard. I knocked at my mum's door and she was shocked to see me home at that time. I was in a state and told her what was being said to me. She told me, "You go straight back to school now and tell them your mother was married when you were born so you are not a bastard! Now get back there and stick up for yourself."

So I did. It didn't go well; they didn't want to hear my explanation, they just wanted to beat me up regardless.

I needed help and was crying out for it and so I turned to the spirit world! I can't remember exactly what got me into them or even the first time I did one but I was bang into Ouija boards, It was a call for help from somewhere, anywhere! I was interested in trying to get in touch with my twin brother who passed before birth. I also had a fixation with the story of the son of Satan 'Damien', only he used to call himself 'Zak' when I believe I reached him. I wanted to see if in the way of a spirit world there was more out there as my mother has always taught me. She says that when I was three years old and I was brushing my teeth at night, when I wandered into her bedroom calmly and said, "Mum, I just see a little boy behind me in the mirror!"

She just told me it was my brother and he was there to protect me and it turns out, he has been, for sure. Time and time again! I remember one day in particular, at junior school, I was being bullied from the moment I had arrived that day and it was planned by a big group of about 20 kids. They had planned to 'get me' at lunchtime on the playing fields. I was petrified and just counting down the minutes all morning long until 12 o'clock rolled around. My best and only friend was Marcus Henry, we stuck together and took the beatings together but this day he wasn't in school. I was alone and felt completely vulnerable and even more open to a beating. So I did something I had never done in school before. I used a Ouija board that I made myself on paper and then I went into the toilets to do it and see if I could contact my brother for help. After about five minutes, I believe I made contact and so I asked for help to stop these boys from beating me up at lunchtime. What was to happen next was proof enough for me that there is a spirit world and my brother resides there ready to look over me and protect me.

The lunch bell rang and my anxieties went through the roof with fear of what was going to happen to me. I queued with my dinner ticket. I got my dinner and I sat alone on a table as close to the teachers as I could get. As I was finishing my dessert (apple crumble and custard) and getting ready to take my tray up, I looked out of the window, the crowd of boys that were waiting to beat me up were all congregating at the corner of the playing field right by a part of the fence that was ripped down leading on to a bush and then the football pitches out the back of my mum's house. I could hear them all shouting my name as if they were shouting at me. What happened next was very strange indeed. I walked out of the doors to the playground after being asked by a teacher to get outside, as I came out a couple of the crowd spotted me. They turned as if they had seen a ghost, their heads back and forth to the bushes then to me. Apparently, they had seen me in the bushes taunting them but then they saw me come through the doors to the playground. They were all shouting at me, "How did you do that?" which, in turn, freaked them all out enough into leaving me alone for the day. I truly believe that they saw my twin brother in the bushes that day, and then saw me behind them all and shat themselves through not understanding what or how it had just happened.

"Thanks, bruv!"

It was also around this time of my life that one of my best mates, 'Jimmy French' stayed over at my mum's for a sleepover. When I awoke in the morning Jimmy was gone. My mother panicked as she was looking after someone else's son and he was missing. So my mum called his mother straight away. His mum informed mine that he arrived home in his pyjamas at four o'clock in the morning (he lived just around the corner) absolutely petrified and saying that he woke up and saw a little boy spirit just sitting on the end of my bed looking at him and laughing. He left without a word in a hurry and he never stepped a foot in the house ever again out of fear. I am still in touch with him to this day and he still maintains the story of the little boy on the bed laughing at him is true and that it really scared him. Nowadays, coming from a broken home is accepted, but when I was a kid in the 80s, everyone had a dad apart from me, it was really hard at times. I wondered why he didn't want to know me. The main biggest bully that I remember was named Davey Legg. He fuckin' terrorised me for years, and I swore to myself to get my own back one day, someway, somehow, and believe me, years and years later I did.

That little cunt needed to get it and get it hard. I wanted to ruin his life the way he had ruined mine, well, what I'd lived of it anyway. So I did. I bided my time (for years) and fucking ruined his life. As the story unfolds, you'll find out how, whether you agree with what I did or not is entirely another thing, but I don't really give a fuck, sorry!! He put me through hell!!

When I was about 12 years of age, I was playing out with the neighbour kids and there was a boy called Micky. He used to race around on a racer bike round and round the cul-de-sac and we all used to chase him and try to catch him. He was not quite the full ticket; he was a loner and used to ride around making weird noises at us. He used to go on long bike rides with a known paedophile, which was half the reason we chased him along with the fact he was a bit backward and he seemed to enjoy it and laugh as he got away on his bike. One day I was chasing this boy, he was a few years older than me, and I was hot on his tail. He was on his bike and I was on foot,

I was so close to catching him as he left the cul-de-sac towards Whitmore way (a main road) as he got further away I gave up and turned away to walk back to where the other kids were waiting and watching. All of a sudden, I heard the screech of tyres very loudly and a massive smashing sound, I turned around to see Micky get hit by a car, he flew about 15ft in the air and the car coming in the opposite direction also hit him forcing him to land face down on a curb stone, smashing his face wide open.

As I watched, I turned white and was sick on the spot, it was horrifying and I instantly felt responsible obviously, but I had stopped chasing him and he just carried on into the road. The ambulance was there within five minutes to try and save him, but he was dead on the road. The paramedics resuscitated Micky and saved him but in the hospital, he fell into a coma, this was bad, within an hour the police were at my mum's to question me about the accident asking me if "it was a malicious attack?" me chasing him and was the aim "to hurt him if I caught him?"

I was so scared as they were talking about a detention centre if he didn't make it. I was looking at a manslaughter charge (7 to 14 years minimum); I needed him to pull through as did his family.

Micky's family had a decision to make. They lived about six doors away, were they going to press charges to have me held in custody until they knew the outcome? I heard the mother wanted to press charges but the father didn't. Weeks and weeks passed with no improvement; it looked like they were going to turn the machines that were keeping Micky alive, off. Shit, prison was the next step for sure. At 12 years old, my life like Micky's in a sense, would be over. But at

19

least I was alive even though I thought to myself, *If I go away I will kill myself.*

A few more weeks passed and a decision was made, they were giving it one more week before turning off the machines and Micky would die. A few days before the deadline, believe it or not, to everybody's amazement and sheer ecstatic pleasure he woke up, he had his life back and I was hoping so did I, but would he ever be the same again? Also would I? I couldn't leave the house through fear of people shouting out "MURDERER, MURDERER," and his friends and family chasing me with weapons threatening to hurt me for what I'd apparently done and throwing rocks at me etc.

I hear unfortunately the accident has effected Micky's brain and his mental age is years behind what it should be. I got over it pretty fucking quickly to be honest as since the bullying and abuse at a younger age, I've been a bit of a horrible cunt as I got older. I blame the situations I'd been put through. Plus, other complications/events in my life lead me to be a nasty cold-hearted bastard If I want to be, I can also be the complete opposite to the right people (the ones that are there for me no matter what!).

As kids We used to go to a place in Basildon called Rollermania. We all used to drink a two-litre bottle of strong cider, like white lightning before we went, have a few joints in the park and then we would get one of our pals who had paid to let us in through the back fire exits to save paying. If we didn't have any money between us, we would do a 'beer run' as we called it, which basically meant you run in a shop grab as much alcohol as you can and you run, but what would this 'petty crime' turn into? We started doing it every Friday night at the same shop called 'Alldays'; there was about eight of us doing it. One would hold the door open so that it couldn't be locked from the inside and the rest of us would grab a whole crate of anything alcoholic and run. We did the same place for about four weeks and then one week we all ran in there on a Friday night, only this time they were ready. As we got to the back of the shop to the fridges (we didn't want warm beer ha) the police came bursting out the back doors at us about twenty strong. A few of the boys got nicked but thank fuck I was quick on my toes and I got away (with the beer). We used to cause carnage in Rollermania kicking off fights all over the place but the marshals were on it to stop it all. One night, I remember me and my mate, Steve came out of Rollermania and we wanted a fight, so I said to Steve, "You kick it off."

He replied, "No, you kick it off."

This went on a few times before I thought *Fuck it*. I shouted at the top of my voice, "Who wants a fucking row then?" Out of about 40 people, one turned around, he was the biggest lad I had ever seen for our age. I thought, *For fucks sake it would be wouldn't it*. He stood there on his skates (which made him about a foot taller and I had my trainers on) and he said, "Yeah, fucking come on then."

I had never seen him before; I ran up to him and threw the first punch to his ribs, this crippled him but he still stood tall, so I went to town on his ribs as he was so tall. My trademark 'rib breaking' had come into play in earlier weeks, I then chased him on foot and he was on his skates, for about two miles before I gave up. Later, I would find out this was the younger brother of somebody everybody our age feared, 'Suge' was his name. He was older than me and one hard bastard. This younger brother of his was named Lenny, and

21

as I had found out who he was, it didn't take him long to find out who I was either. He went around to one of our mutual friend's house (though we didn't know it at the time), and he said to him, "Some fucker done me last night at Rollermania."

Jay, (the friend) asked Lenny, "What happened?"

Lenny went on to lift up the top he was wearing and showed Jay his mid-section. Jay took one look and like a grass said straight away, "That's Fisher bruv; he does peoples ribs." My reason for attacking the rib area was thus, one, with the severe blows I was delivering with my fists and tools etc, if I had hit the head it would have resulted in death and two, the pain I had inflicted was personal, I didn't need others to see it, including any of those nosey coppers that might want to ask what happened, you never know.

Now, at school, this Jay was what you would call 'a boffin'. I mean seriously this fella was as straight as they come. The fucking headmaster could have trusted him with his wife and his life as he was so into school. He would never miss a day even if he was ill, his answer would be to go to school and get through it. He didn't mix with our lot as he didn't agree with what we were doing (the drugs etc). He just loved school and was really going places when he left. Or was he? You know what, certain drugs can get ANYBODY!!! He is hard evidence now. I'm not sure if he is still alive. Let's just say he looked like he was on death's door the last time I saw him and was addicted to heroin.

Moving on, I worked from a young age and was hungry for money. I wanted nice things and I wanted my girlfriend to have nice things, and despite my young age I was working on the market first at 4 o'clock in the morning about four days a week (I loved it). Then on to two paper rounds on my roller skates and all this was before school. It was all cash in hand and obviously illegal. But back then it was the done thing, I was only twelve years old, the school soon cottoned on to what I was doing when I was regularly late on the same days of the week every week, and so I was forced to stop or the school was going to report it. I don't think this helped at all in stopping me going down a slippery darker road of crime and drugs for money at any hour. I would later become a magnet for crime and drug dealers.).

I also washed cars at the weekend for more money, and this was a real good earner if you did a good job. There is still really good money in it to this day! You see the car washes everywhere nowadays as nobody seems to want to do it themselves. I had about seven cars every other Saturday, and one house I went to, the geezer had four minibuses, some weekends six of them, he wanted them all done EVERY Saturday without fail. I can't remember what I used to charge but as you can imagine this was a lovely little earner for a 12-year-old (from one job). And this was a regular income so I was used to having my own money from a very young age. This is good right?? The thing is…this helped to contribute in sending me down the WRONG path because believe it or not, I now had 'a thirst for cash'.

My life of crime and drugs started at the age of 12ish and I would one day become known locally as 'the son of the devil' and my mum would be branded 'a witch'. I would be mocked by a few but feared by many. It started with just hiding in the bushes and smoking normal cigarettes and drinking any alcohol we could find or pinch from our parents' drinks cupboard and then it swiftly moved on to solid cannabis but we used to call it 'draw'.

One cloudy day, I was hiding around the back of my mum's house by the football sheds which was also a boxing club including a ring etc. It was quite a big building made entirely of wood. A pal and I were around there having a crafty fag out of sight. I was playing with a new windproof lighter I had just acquired from my mum on the quiet. My pal asked to have a look and was stupidly lighting a little piece of paper poking out from a slat of wood on the building. I blew it out, or so I thought I did. We had finished our fag and started to walk across the other mass of fields. As we walked for about ten minutes, we looked back and there was just a mass of thick black smoke billowing from the field where we had just been. I put two and two together rather quickly and did a runner and didn't look back. I ran for miles in a panic from the damage I, or HE, had accidentally caused and was anybody inside? I ran to a friend a few miles from my mum's house to stay well away. When I got home later that evening my mum said to me, "You missed all the action someone burnt down the boxing club."

I just acted shocked; my mum doesn't know to this day that it was me and him. Sorry, mum. There was also a model train club in the building which was destroyed in the totalling fire costing tens of thousands of pounds so the local news said. I later heard that the building was lined with polystyrene so the smouldering paper must have caught alight to the inside of the building and it was gone in minutes. It really was an accident though.

One night, I was out with my pals, Slick, Gav, Greg and a few others. We were round Greg's house and his parents were out for the evening so we got the decks out started pumping the music and having a smoke of draw that I was now doing regularly. Now, I used to smoke puff but tonight I was going to get stitched up in a big way. The boys got three Coca-Cola two litre bottles, they cut the top off of one and the bottom off of another with one in the middle with both top and bottom off acting as a tube in the middle. These bottles were tapped together to create one large six litre contraption. This was a monster bottle. Slick, without me knowing, put £15 worth of cannabis in to burn. We released the water into the bath and the bottle filled with smoke. How it was done will be explained.

Slick forced me to suck it all up even though I was being sick at the same time and in a fit of coughing. So I had done it. So, what? We all went for a walk to the shop for some food as we were all stoned but as we got about half-way to the shop, I wasn't feeling right. The shop was about a five-minute walk but by the time I got there, I felt sick and could hardly walk or even see; I had never felt like this before. The boys sat me in a doorway opposite the shops whilst they went to get food and drink to try and sober me up. By now, I was bringing up blood, just pumping it up. I looked up and all my mates were dressed as clowns and using funny voices like the clown 'Pennywise' from the film 'IT'. They were all putting food in my face, just these big long arms coming at me from all angles. I completely freaked out. I was a pale shade of green. The boys picked me up and took me home to my mum's house; they knocked at the door and got on their toes double lively, leaving me slumped against the front door. As my mum opened the door I just fell through it into her arms, At least they did the right thing in the end, huh? I think my mum thought I was drunk as I just went straight up to bed until the next evening. I slept the whole next day. Would I go back and do it all again? Well...

When I was young I also had a great fascination/fixation with the criminal underworld and completely besotted with people like the Krays, the Richardson's, Roy Shaw, 'the Guvnor' Lenny Mclean, Roy 'pretty boy' Shaw etc, even Pat Tate and Tony Tucker (the Essex boys) took my fancy. This was just the beginning of a lot of pure evil madness as notoriety is something I always craved, but there are thousands of people out there that would do anything to get out of the life that I was trying so desperately to get in to. Now, if you have never heard of me then I obviously didn't get it, but then again if you're reading this book...then I might still of yet.

I wanted to be like them so much that I would put myself into that world of danger to try and get there. I'd say I was almost obsessed by them all, who knew 20 years later I would become the best of friends with the deceased Pat Tate's nephew, Allun Tate. We are really close and look out for each other and it has nothing to do with crime.

. I would do anything to help 'little Al Tate' out and we speak about three or four times a day.

Back in my school years, I'd generally be with my best mate Luke Nevendon. He was just so witty and funny and made me laugh all day every day; he was just coming out with sayings and catchphrases every few minutes. Lukey and I were as close as two best mates could be, it was great, and at school, I was part of a crowd, the 'in crowd' if you like. In the first few months of high school, we were so naughty in school that the school rearranged our year to split us, naughty boys, up. I had to carry a report card around with me so each teacher from each lesson could comment on my behaviour that period. I lost my report card so often (or threw it away) that in the end my tutor sellotaped the report card onto an extra-large piece of wood so that I wouldn't lose it... I just found this comical as oppose to embarrassing. It just attracted attention and let's face it, when we are at that age that's all we want, okay, some of us more than others but still.

I'd been at senior school for a while now and would not be bullied anymore. I couldn't take it again but I was waiting for it none the less. One day, not long after starting high school, a boy started on me in the corridor and I froze for a split second, as I was not tooled up, before a boy two years above me came over to help me and just belted this bully square on the chin and put him on his arse out cold I looked...and I thought wow that looked easy so the next time someone got lemon with me and I felt under threat I just simply spanked them hard on the jaw... He went down and got up and ran off. Oooh, I got a taste for it now!!!

Let's fucking have it!!!

I had a girlfriend and she was the most popular girl in the year and everyone was after her including boys from the years above, but she loved a bad boy and I was the 'baddest boy' in the year all of a sudden and also considered one of the hardest to fight, for my age. I was not about to be bullied ever again and I had a reputation to build for the future and keep it up for reasons still not entirely clear to me. We had an ice cream van on the school premises on our early break. There was never a queue, just a mob of about 40 kids all pushing and shoving to get their sweets. Ha, funny really, drug addicts act the same around the dealer's car when it pulls up. Anyway I used to wait to hear someone put a £2 to £5 order in (which was generally the biggest) and I would hide in the front of the mob but crouching down and as the sweets and money were passed I would do my best to grab both, (the sweets and the money) and if I didn't get the money I would sell the sweets, well at least half of them for double the price . Even at home, I was on the scam. My mum had a BT payphone and it was set on a high number four setting so when the bill came in she always had four times the money but I was picking the lock with a hairpin and swiping handfuls of pound coins for months and no one ever noticed (sorry, mum).

I used to meet up with a pal whose name was 'Billy Wells' and we would get stoned before school. The way Billy and I met was…well…you could say 'awkward' and 'tense' to say the least. One night after school, I met up with a mate of mine named Kev; I think I was around about 12 or 13 years old. He said to me, "Fisher, there's a new boy starting at your school tomorrow, he's in your year. Do NOT fuck with him he's a fucking nutter, and he's as hard as they come, trust me."

I took offence to this as I considered myself one of the hardest in my year; I'd fight anyone these days and I had a reputation to keep up. Being in our playground at lunchtime was like a fucking prison courtyard sometimes. It was kicking off everywhere more or less every day. The rock in a sock was a favourite amongst the older lot, people were forever whipping them out of their backpacks and chasing someone to attack them, it was mental. So I followed suit and carried one myself from a very young age. I did not care or even consider the damage this weapon could do, especially if taken to the head, fuck it!

Anyway back to meeting Billy Wells, I went home that night after meeting Kev and thought, *Well, I'd better go in tooled up.* So I went down to big Q chip shop on Whitmore Way in Basildon and kicked out a perfectly round cobble from the ground by the side of the road, I took it home and put it in a sock. I actually wrapped the cobble in a single sock and then put it in another sock to swing (this cuts the chances of the sock splitting when you hit someone). If I'm being honest, I was nervous about the next day at school, as I say I had a reputation to uphold and I was facing someone I'd been warned about which was unusual in its self as my mates knew what I was capable of and I could now look after myself. So I went to my most trusted friend for advice, Lukey Nevendon. He'd heard of Billy Wells! Shit!! This was bad. He agreed with Kev and said I should steer clear, what the fuck was I going to do? The anxiety was definitely kicking in now.

The next morning rolled around, I woke up and the first thing on my mind was Billy Wells…*today's the day…* I got up and got dressed as normal, only this morning I was tooling up in the frame of mind that could have resulted in an accidental or premeditated murder. The 'rock in a sock was tucked into my trousers with the end hanging over the top of my trousers and into my right-hand pocket with my tucked-in shirt just about hanging over it so it could not be seen and was at hand and easy to whip out quickly if needed. This day was a big deal to me. Was I going to get done or would I beat him? Because I knew, either way, it was going to kick off between me and him as we both had something to prove. He was the 'new boy' and I was the so-called hardest in the year so…

What's good for nerves? I thought to myself as quarter past eight came around. Alcohol, yeah let's try that. So I raided my mum's alcohol cupboard and mixed 'Pernod', 'vodka', 'Bacardi', 'whisky', 'brandy' and a few other random drinks in a two-litre Coca-Cola bottle. I filled it about half-way and topped it up with coke. I left the house pretty sharpish and downed as much of this vile alcoholic lethal cocktail as I could on the walk across the fields to school; I was fucking up for anything by now. I got to school and went straight to my form room which is where the register would be held every day. Would Billy Wells be in my class? No, he wasn't, my form tutor was also the Spanish teacher. My first class incidentally was Spanish on the day so I didn't need to move, another class would be joining us, a new boy walked in and sat down opposite me, it must be Billy, he glared at me with a wandering eye, he had a skin head but personally I didn't think he looked hard or tough. I looked him in the eye and said, "What the fuck are you looking at, ya mug?"

He replied simply, "YOU ya cunt."

I thought, *Shit, he's up for it and don't give a shit.* But I would NEVER back down, so I said to him, "You fucking little prick, I'll smash your fucking head in."

Billy came back at me with, "Lets fucking have it then… after this lesson, you dick head."

I wasn't fussed I was at boiling point and quite drunk, plus I had my tool as back up. The rest of the lesson was tense; if looks could kill, I'd be a dead man (then again so would everyone else have been with that wandering eye of his). The teacher clocked what was going on between me and Billy and at the end of the lesson, she held him back until she knew I was in my next class. As the day dragged on I didn't bump into Billy at all, so I carried on as normal but there was a lot of hype and talk of me and him fighting at lunchtime or after school. The end of the day came and I was feeling anxious. I was leaving school out the back way as normal to cross the four fields to get home. As I opened the door at the rear end of the school, Billy was stood there, I thought, *Here we go!*

I put my hand on my tool and approached him. As I got closer to him my heart was pounding and I was building myself up in my head for a fight, but then as I got even closer to him he said to me, "Oi, do you smoke?"

I said, "Yeah."

He replied, "But do you smoke puff?"

I said, "Yeah, why?"

He reached in his pocket and pulled out the biggest lump of draw (cannabis resin) I'd ever seen at the time. It was a nine-ounce bar.

He said to me, "Let's go and have a smoke."

So off we went to his house together and we got absolutely smashed. His mother knew and let him/us smoke in his bedroom. The room was a typical 'smoker's room'; there were Bob Marley flags draped from the ceiling and posters all over the walls including the man Bob and loads of flyers from raves like world dance and Helter Skelter – he had them all. I mean the place was covered. It was a place you could really chill. It was the bollox. A dangerous friendship was forming though, one that would spiral out of control with mind-bending drugs, alcohol, petty crime and serious violence. Court cases would be imminent, but to be honest, I was excited by this and didn't give a fuck! We got on like a house on fire and Billy introduced me to LSD and ecstasy and we were taking LSD tabs and ecstasy in school. The teachers knew something was wrong but back then they wouldn't suspect we would be doing that for one second. We were too young...right? Wrong...

Our school was so shit and unruly we literally used to get up in the middle of a lesson and walk out and nothing would be said, apart from one teacher who used to pin me to the wall and scream in my face that I was a 'bloody parasite' (his words). Teachers used to watch us from the windows on the school ground taking drugs (smoking weed and draw) and never stopped us; they even filmed us one time and threatened to call the police. Huh, what a joke (crack on with that, you mugs).

After a while, I got a little crew together and started arranging fights in the town centre on a Friday night at the age of 12 or 13. We would approach Macdonald's and if there was a crowd there, it was on. We would take our belts off and wrap them around our hands with the buckle hanging ready to fucking hurt someone. You had the buckle to hit them with but also the leather of the belt wrapped around your hand would act as protection for your knuckles when you punch someone hard. My pal, who we called Spud, always kicked it off first even though he was the smallest of us, but he knew we were about 15 strong and tooled up to the eyeballs and fucking ready for a tear up. Within seconds, there would be 25 to 30 kids kicking the shit out of each other and we fucking loved it. It was like a turf war tear up at a football match just on a much smaller scale, –oh and we never lost.

I was a fan of using gas first and either my belt or a rock in a sock to finish them, 'gas em' and smash em'' or part of a bannister I cut down and used as a cosh as it was the perfect shape (like a small rounder's bat) very light but used to split heads with a good hit. One night it all kicked off with a crowd of about eight or nine people, remember that this is BASED on true events and may be exaggerated and fabricated in ways for dramatisation. It ended up with one left standing he had a hold of my pal so one of our lot ran up and belted him knocking him clean out. He got up within seconds and thought it was me. He came at me like a fucking animal, looking like he was going to kill me, so I whipped out my cosh and fucking lumped him straight over the head with it, he hit the floor so I made sure he didn't get up again. I broke all his ribs while my pal was literally jumping on his head, he was lying in a big pool of blood as we left; he would later fall into a coma.

I was arrested trying to escape the area; six of us got pinched (arrested). The police saw from a distance the weapon get tossed into the bush from us four but didn't see who it was that threw it, so they retrieved it and a friend of mine, since I was a baby, was the one to grass me up for what I had done and for having the weapon used but because mine and the other four's stories were the same I got released. The boy who bubbled me up didn't come out of his house for around a year through fear of bumping into me and getting fucking hurt. It did go to court but was thrown out due to lack of evidence, thank fuck!! I was bound over to keep the peace. I think that's enough information on that one (too much will get me shot). I could have been looking at an attempted murder charge and I was only about 13. This was the second person I had put in a coma, the third was a different story.

Billy and I were sitting in his bedroom smoking weed and drinking beer, we may have taken a pill or two (ecstasy) I don't remember as necking anything became totally normal to me, literally second nature. It was a Saturday night and it was Billy's birthday, together, Billy and I were fucking dangerous, we just wanted to instil fear into anyone and everyone that heard of us, and everybody that knew us.

Bill said to me, "Let's go out to town and kick the fuck out of someone."

I said, "Yeah, but who?"

Billy said, "Johnny owes me a tenner, that's enough of a reason for me, lets fucking find him."

Johnny was a close friend to Bill but he didn't give a shit he just wanted to hurt someone and to be honest, so did I. I was getting excited, so I said, "Do you know where he's going to be right now?"

Billy replied, "I'll call him and find out he won't suspect a thing."

It turned out he was in Basildon town centre (my fucking playground), it was on!!! We downed another couple of beers and a few shots of Jack Daniels, we got tooled up with a can of CS gas and a rock in a sock each, we were not necessarily going to need them but if other people were to jump in we knew we could take them on with the tools. We left Billy's house in Laindon, it was about a 20-minute walk to the town so we had another couple of beers on the way. Bill called Johnny and told him to wait there as if we were just meeting him for a Saturday night get together like normal, he did not know what was coming!! We got to the town, we saw Johnny and approached him, Billy said, under his breath with his head down, "Watch this, I'm gonna knock him out with my left hand."

Bill shouted aggressively to Johnny, "Where's my fucking money, you cunt?"

Johnny realised all of a sudden that Bill was not fucking about. Johnny shat himself and said in a panic, "My sister is coming now with your tenner, bruv, I swear, right now."

Billy just said to him, "It's too late mate," and he belted him with his left hand and knocked him clean out for a few seconds. To Johnny's credit, he was straight back on his feet throwing and trading punches with Bill and it was a good fight. I thought Johnny might be getting the better of Billy and Bill then called for my help as he couldn't seem to evade the punches for long enough to grab a 'tool'. So I jumped in and started punching Johnny in the ribcage as this had become my 'trademark' over the years. I broke quite a few of his ribs whilst Billy was trading punches with him to the head, after about five minutes Johnny hit the floor and gave up but we didn't stop. Billy was jumping on his head and I was hitting him in to break his ribs; we left him in a pool of blood (fuck not another one). There were about four young girls screaming at us, "You've killed him, you've killed him," so we ran and we thought that was that for now but what would come of it? Was he dead? The next day we heard Johnny had fallen into a coma. FOR FUCK'S SAKE, we were shitting ourselves. Or at least I was, Billy was about as cool as a fucking tub of Ben and Jerry's in an igloo. Anyway, a few days passed and we heard nothing, thinking we had got away with it, knowing machines were keeping Johnny alive, but if the witnesses had said anything we would have been nicked by now surely. Anyway, a week passed and Saturday rolled around again, I woke up to two coppers standing in my bedroom at the end of my bed shaking my leg and calling my name, *Fuck I'm in shit big time.*

I knew through a friend of Johnny's sister he was still on life support. Anyway, I was obviously arrested and dragged out in my boxer shorts and a t-shirt with my tracksuit bottoms in my hand behind my back cuffed so I couldn't even put them on. I was bundled up into the car at half eight in the morning in front of all the neighbours once again. I was put through the usual shit, kept in the cells for 23 hours and interviewed at the last minute. The police hated me because of my surname (Slaven). My biological father was very well known to the old bill and spent more than half of his entire life at her majesty's pleasure and being my father, they all assume I see him and that we are close. I was given a court date and I was worried, to say the least. I didn't fancy jail. The court date was about a month away and we needed Johnny to wake up to at least lessen our charges from another attempted murder or manslaughter to GBH and/or ABH which still carried a sentence of around four years at the time. I thought I was fucked and going down (prison).

Johnny woke up after a few weeks just before the court case. We still had to worry about the witnesses, four young girls, what the fuck were we going to do? These girls knew us and knew our names. The court case came around too quickly for my liking, I thought I was going to prison for sure, but we got to court and thanks to the spirits that look after me, somebody apparently intimidated the witnesses and they dropped out and never showed at court so it was also thrown out. This was another very lucky escape from going to young offender's once again, and I didn't even need to get my hands dirty, someone was looking out for me. By the end of this 'mostly, true story' you will wonder how on earth I haven't ended up DEAD or at least 'locked up permanently'. I'm still wondering myself as it gets worse, a lot worse.

I don't remember exactly how old I was but there was a massive group of us over at Gloucester park lakes one time 'night fishing'. I really don't remember names or much about that messy night getting out of our nuts at the lakes, but I do remember this. There was a small group of girls in the group we were in, all-around two tents, and after an hour or so we started to talk to a group of lads in another tent about twenty paces from where we were set up. I wasn't actually fishing. I know nothing about fishing to this very day, I was just there to take drugs and get drunk. One of the girls all of a sudden started freaking out and crying hysterically and mumbling something frantically to herself under breath as her head turned rapidly from side to side almost as if she was possessed for a minute. She was in a bad way. It took me a while to calm her down but when I eventually did I was about to hear something I did not want to hear. This young girl (under 13!) told me the bloke in the next tent tried raping her a few weeks prior. As soon as I heard this, I went crazy, and within seconds, I am in the next tent dragging this fucking scumbag out. He started to try to fight me, so I punched him hard on the jaw, knocking him delirious as he was drugged up to the eyeballs on smack by the looks of him. I dragged him kicking and waving his arms about over to the lake and I grabbed him by the hair and I plunged his head into the freezing cold filthy lake. I held him in for about ten seconds and I knew he was struggling to breathe from the air bubbles coming up to the surface but he was weak and easy to hold under. I pulled him up and screamed at him, "What the fuck did you do? Come on, you cunt, tell me what you fucking done!!"

He was clueless as to what I was talking about so I put him in the water again by the hair. I repeated this about five times until he was gasping for air and trying to ask me to stop but he couldn't get the words out (he must have been frightened). After, I called the girl over and made him beg for her forgiveness and get on his knees, and he did. She didn't accept and she ran back to our camp still crying. I hadn't made it better for her but I was showing her she had support although I didn't even know her. This sort of thing is close to my heart for certain reasons that did not surface until I was 26 years old. Then it would become clear why I couldn't stand this type of story (sexual abuse) it would flip my switch in every case no matter who the victim. I would do ANYTHING I could to help (not that I felt I really could) but I did humiliate people in my past for doing things that they shouldn't have done to other people, but even though I did this, I don't know if it ever helped. It's surprising how many people you meet that have been sexually assaulted as a child or at some point in their life. It really is shocking.

With the type of people I was mixing with, it was no wonder I would end up violent. One of my very close pals at the time (Dave) was just leaving the pub there was about 10 of us at the jolly friar in Basildon and it was new year's eve. We had been invited to a party on Craylands estate, Basildon (another of my playgrounds where I felt safe to be a naughty fucker and play up). Three blokes a lot older than us staggered out of the pub shouting at the top of their voices at us, saying, "Where the fuck are you lot going?"

So Dave replied, "We're going to a party mate you're not invited!"

The blokes continued to say they were 'coming with us' and they were just generally being aggressive and threatening towards us all treating us like little kids; boy, were they in for a shock. We didn't take to kindly to that sort of thing, and each and every one of us felt the same and would respect each other's principles and beliefs. So, we started walking and they walked with us. Dave had taken his pint glass from the pub and walked off with it down the hill. As we were walking, one bloke in particular (the lippy bloke) said to Dave, "So, where we going fat boy?"

Dave just said, "FAT BOY?"

He looked over at me and gave me a crafty wink and a smile as he sunk the rest of his drink and without saying a word he smashed the bloke clean in the face with his pint glass, and I mean it was angled at such a way it was as if the fella was about to drink from the glass (not flat) done for maximum impact and maximum damage. The geezer was cut up bad to the extent where he needed plastic surgery to look vaguely back to the way he originally looked and he put a reward out on whoever it was that done it (that's why I've changed the name). Out of the three of them, the one that got glassed did a runner and so did one of his mate's but one stayed for the fight thinking he was tough even after seeing what he had just witnessed with his pal. I started to rip apart a brown wooden picket fence and smashing the geezer with a plank of wood with nails in it. Everybody (even the girls) followed suit and started pulling planks off of the fence to do the fella in. In the end, he curled up in a ball whilst we all beat him for being so fucking cocky and he bled from all places. Someone shouted, "police," so we all jumped onto a garden behind bushes and all laid there flat on the floor as the bushes were only about 2ft tall all the way around us and watched the police very slowly creep past us all with the side spotlights shining brightly above us, they were on the hunt for us. We had slipped through that one by the skin of our fucking teeth. The lesson there? Don't get fucking lemon with one of us.

We were like travellers, we came in numbers, we came in hard and we stuck together and if you started on one, then you would get done. Simple.

I was about 13 years old, maybe younger when I really heavily started taking the speed and Ecstasy. I'd been dabbling in it with Billy Wells for a while. The fighting had got boring and the puff just wasn't cutting it anymore, I wanted a stronger buzz. My best mate Luke was on every class 'A' available, he would take anything just like me, he said he'd be able to look after me if I should have a bad trip on a pill or something or if I fell into a 'k hole' from the ketamine pills, he could look after me. We were really close so I trusted him with my life and took whatever he gave me knowing (or thinking) it would turn into a good laugh every time. I had been smoking solid and bud with him for years, for a much bigger hit (buzz) than a joint we used to put tin foil on the top of a two-litre bottle (remember, like the one that stitched me up) with big dip in it with holes in. We put a small drain hole in the bottom of the bottle, fill it up with water and put your bud in the top, as you burn it and let the water go it sucks in the pure smoke, once the water is drained and the bottle is full of smoke you simply suck it all up in one go, now that gets you stoned more than any joint will ever get you. I don't recommend it.

One day I sucked up two or three bottles with my pal in the space of a couple of hours and I said to him, "Bruv, I got the munchies bad. I'm going to pop indoors and grab something to eat."

He told me I looked smashed and my eyes were glazed and bloodshot and so if I went in, my mum would clock on that I was stoned because my eyes were so red, but against my pals better judgment I went in. He was right my mum took one look at me and screamed, "What the hell are you on?"

I denied it but she could blatantly see it, she told me I was grounded for a month and I was banned from hanging around with Luke – yeah right, like that was going to stop me. I think the grounding lasted about two weeks and my mum had had enough of me in the house and so she allowed me out. What was the first thing I did? Go straight round Lukey's to suck up a massive bottle in his bathroom of course. Yeah... Love it... Luke's parents knew what we were doing but they allowed it under the impression that if we were doing it indoors, we wouldn't get nicked on the streets doing it. Another one was the 'brain bucket' we cut the bottom off of a big bottle and filled a bucket up with water, as you pull the bottle up and burn the weed in the top the bottle fills with smoke, you simply push your head down with your mouth around the top of the bottle after removing the foil and 'bang' the smoke is gone and your lungs are full, again like the bottle, the effects are the same, powerful.

Luke was a year older than me and he had a brother a year younger than me, so we were all together a lot just getting as fucked as we possibly could. One night, Luke and I took LSD (they were little paper tabs with the Rolling stones logo (big mouth/lips) and they were called 'Mick Jagger's'. I put one of these tiny little pieces of paper in my mouth and sucked on it for about ten minutes before chewing it up and swallowing it. I thought what the hell could it possibly do, it's just a bit of paper and I've done it before, right? How wrong could I be? EVERY trip is VERY different. We were in Luke's bedroom and I started coming up on this 'acid trip'. Shit, the walls were bending and all sorts but I was finding it all the funniest thing I had ever seen. I mean I was in hysterics with laughter to the point my stomach and my jaw were aching from laughing so hard and for so long. We decided that it would be a good idea to find somewhere colourful and full of bright lights... Huh, Southend seemed like a plan... But how would we get there with no money? We had just spent our only tenner between us on LSD. I know, we'll bunk the train. We can go to Pitsea train station and go into the fields and jump the fence onto the platform, sounds easy right? I had done it plenty of times sober but try doing it tripping off your face on LSD...

It was about a twenty-minute walk normally but it took us over an hour to get there. We were in a right old 'two an eight' (state), I was carrying three cans of Stella Artois (lager) and by the time we got near the train station, I had one left. I was calling it, 'my lonesome Stella', 'the ole faithful'. I had fallen in love with this can of beer. I was hugging it and kissing it and telling it I loved it, all the time pissing myself with laughter – Oh, this was great fun! I loved laughing so much, anything or anyone that made me laugh I clung on to dearly. We approached the station trying desperately not to laugh at absolutely nothing so we didn't stand out as we slipped down the side of the station into the farmer's fields to try and jump the fence or find a hole in it. We walked along the field a bit and watched out for guards on the platform, we waited until it was clear and we climbed the fence and got over onto the platform, they must have had cameras because guards came from everywhere at once shouting at us, I was still laughing hard, we jumped back over the fence and the 'acid trip' kicked in again HARD; we just didn't know what to do. The answer was easy, all we had to do was go back the way we came and quickly but we thought 'no' we'll walk along all the farmer's fields to Southend (it's about twenty miles). We walked about sixty paces and all of a sudden we didn't know what we were doing there or where we were supposed to be going. We were hiding in a thick muddy deep trench out of sight to anybody, or so we thought, if we'd have stayed low we might have gotten away with it but for some reason, I had the urge to throw my 'lonesome Stella' in the air and watch it hit the soggy mud. It was just so funny to me, every time the full (closed) can hit the mud I would fall over with stomach crippling laughter because of the noise it was making I think. I was in a mess! About fifteen minutes passed and we had weighed up what to do. We couldn't carry on on the fields through fear of being shot by the farmer who owned the land and we couldn't go back over the fence because of the guards, our only choice was to finally come to the conclusion that we needed to go back the way we came. So, as we climbed out of the trench we looked and where we entered the field stood a police officer with an Alsatian 'shit' what now? Fuck it RUN. So we started to run across the fields and the copper shouted, "Stop or I'll let the dog go."

So Luke said, "We've gotta stop bruv, that fucking dog will have us mate."

So we stopped and put our hands up, all the time I'm giggling under my breath, I couldn't help it, I was tripping hard. We stopped and stood still as instructed, the copper said to us, "What the hell are you doing? This is private land!"

I simply replied, "I dunno mate."

He said, "Follow me to the car so I can take your details." As we were walking behind him, I was now laughing aloud again, the copper said over his shoulder, "You been taking drugs?"

I replied, "I'm out of my fucking nut, mate."

Luke said to me, "SHUT UP."

The copper thought Lukey was talking to him, he spun around in a flash and threw his fluorescent coat on the floor and screamed in Luke's face, "You fucking what son? You fucking want it? I got CS gas, an extendable baton and a dog here and we are in the middle of a fucking field where no one will see us!"

Luke shit himself and just said, "Sorry, sorry, I wasn't talking to you officer I swear, I was talking to him."

The copper picked up his coat and marched us to the car (I still can't stop laughing). Anyway, we just gave him some mickey mouse names to run through the computer (before the days of fingerprint machines). I always used a boy's name from school who I knew had never been in trouble); it was a lot easier to 'blag' a copper back then. We were on our way within minutes, our mission had failed but never mind. ha, ta, ta!

We went to our mates' house, two brothers named Dan and Dave. They were both older than me, Dave was a lot older and Dan was just a year or two older. These boys lived like tramps. Dan used to piss in pint glasses and leave them on his windowsill for months till they went mouldy even. It fucking stunk in there and what made it worse (as if you could) it was only one lanky stride to the toilet from his bedroom. They lived with their parents but to be honest they were just as bad. The dad, 'BIG DAVE' Senior thought he was a proper hardcore gangster and he's passed on now so I will not speak ill of the dead but he was a plum. 'Plastic gangster' he sold a bit of pure speed and thought he was a big boy for it (most of the time it was ME that was supplying him, huh, prat!). I don't really remember much of that night after then, all I know is we turned up and they were having a party so me, Luke and two girls we'd picked up (whose names I could never tell you just for the sheer fact that I can't remember them) along the way snuck into the kitchen and went to the fridge, we took every beer in there, a bit of munch and left sharpish before anyone clocked that we had gone. I haven't a clue after that! Probably back to Luke's mum's house as we could do pretty much anything in there if his dad wasn't there or was in bed. His mum was very liberal and I'd go as far as to say I think she found it funny seeing us out of our nuts and all over the place (quite bad when I look back). She saw it as, "if we were off the streets doing all sorts" at least we couldn't get arrested being in there I suppose. We just drunk the beers we had pinched from the party and carried on having a smoke then as I say what happened after that is any one's guess.

A few days later, Luke and I were discussing my surname 'Fisher'.

I said to Luke (my best mate for a long time), "Fisher's not my name, my real name ya prat it's Slaven."

He said "WHAT? I know a Brian Slaven, he is where I get all my drugs from. He can't be your old man, he's off his fucking rocker bruv! I mean the geezer is one of the hardest blokes in the town, mate. He's absolutely nuts!"

I had even waited around the corner from this bloke's house because no one was allowed in that he didn't know. Ha, he was my DAD! "so called". So... There was now to be a big long-lost loving reunion yeah? Huh, nope. Luke was too scared to mention me to Brian as Brian was a known psychopath and was known to absolutely flip at the smallest of things and with ANYBODY. Luke was not up for the risk of getting his face cut or smashed in or even getting killed. Yes, Brian was that bad. Unpredictable, volatile and dangerous! As I would say, 'not quite wired right'. Brian WAS to come into my life but it wasn't to be now and the circumstances wouldn't be great when I finally did meet with him having no other choice but to do so.

So… my days of heavy/serious crime were about to start here!

Luke took me to a place called 'Cranes Court' a few times. The local newspapers ended up calling it the 'Bronx of Basildon' after a good friend of mine killed someone in a drug deal gone wrong, a story I don't know too much about just like I told CID when they pulled me in. After a bloody good run in this place, this incident would spell the end of this 'money train base camp' for us all (another story to come). This place would become my hub for a couple of years and hundreds of thousands of pounds would pass through my hands, maybe even millions.

We were hanging around in some random girl's flat. We just took over in there, it was just somewhere to go and get out of our nuts out of sight of the old bill. This place was fucked up! Everybody just popping pills and taking amounts of speed like you wouldn't believe, I fucking loved it. But though I was into taking drugs, because I had always, or from a young age, had money, I was always dressed immaculately. I usually wore either smart designer jeans or trousers and a finely pressed shirt with cufflinks and I spent money on clothes every single week and made sure I was clean and well presented (it comes from my dear passed grandad). Well, anyway, this place may as well have had a revolving door because people were in and out all day and night, every day and every night, at all hours; it was a fucking free for all.

There were some big bastards coming and going and deals forever being done in the kitchen, accompanied by holdalls of cash and massive amounts of pills being handed over. Over a period of time, I heard a few names mentioned that I'd heard before when friends had been talking about the London gangster scene and books they had read. If I'm honest this excited me as I was obsessed with being feared first and rich along with it was an aim of mine. Being young and naive, I wanted to prove myself to the elders, and having a monkey (£500) in my pocket was like winning the lottery for a day as I knew I would have it all again by tomorrow night, which in its own way made me even more dangerous because I'd do anything for the money.

It was not a long time to pass before I was selling ecstasy and speed paste (amphetamine). This stuff was as pure as it comes; it was fucking rocket fuel, it was also called 'base'. I started getting 'powder power' (arrogant); the drugs and the money were going to my head. I thought I was invincible and couldn't be touched as I worked for people that were hugely feared throughout the Essex underworld, even the police stayed away from cranes court where I mainly worked. I don't care what anyone says they were shitting themselves. If any of our crowd caught wind of anybody else selling in cranes court estate we went straight through their doors at night by kicking them clean off. Before kicking the door I would shout, "KNOCK, KNOCK, WAKEY, WAKEY," then 'BANG' the fucking door would go through and we took whatever drugs they had and gave them a fucking good kicking and this was just a warning. They were told never to sell anything on the estate without buying it from us and even then, they had to sell it elsewhere. This was a tactic that would shoot me up the ranks and I would become a sought-after boy to have on the payroll, or at least on your fucking team because you didn't want to go against me. I was fourteen and I was going to take over the place! I was the 'door kicker'. I was the first face the new dealer would see, and I didn't bother trying to hide my face either. I wanted people to know it was me. This way I would build a reputation through fear and also gain respect from the bosses. Even if a car pulled up that didn't belong to one of our lot or a customer for one of us, then every window would be smashed and the stereo would be taken along with anything in the glove compartment but it was also to get a point across to stay away unless you were there to deal with us. If you didn't come to buy from us you left losing out somehow. Cranes Court consisted of only about 30 bedsits; we used about five of them for bases where we would sell from, hide drugs and use as 'safe houses'.

I remember one day I had been out on the streets selling and I just walked into Hayley's flat (one of our bases). I had about fifteen pills and a bag of speed left from work (nothing really but enough for a sentence in jail). As I walked in, I stashed the drugs in a coat that was hanging up. 'BANG, BANG, BANG' on Hayley's door. We heard, "It's the police, open the door."

Hayley shouted out, "Fuck off, who is it?" thinking it was someone messing about.

They repeated, "It's the police" so 'H' opened the door and the old bill stormed in and they said they were looking for Scott Fisher also known as, Slaven. They took one look at me sat on a chair to their right and as I fitted the description they had, they dragged me outside and leaned me over a railing with one copper holding my hands and two others searching me. Bloody close call; I had only just stashed the pills and speed in someone else's jacket literally seconds before. They were not found, I was in luck!!! Even if they had been found, it wasn't my coat so I weren't too fussed. The police asked why I had an amount of cash on me and I told them I'd been working on the market setting up and I'd been saving. I had actually been working for cash in hand for my stepdad, Colin. I was still living at home but also staying in the bases a lot, working (selling drugs). I had no outgoings and with the combination of earning as a tiler and selling pills etc, I felt like I was fucking rolling in money. I was earning £80 cash in hand tiling and on a slow night, I'd take £300, more or less in PROFIT, from the E's and the speed without leaving my 'base'. As the money rolled in, the girls sprung up from everywhere, even older women wanted to know me. I had a reputation as a fucking nutter and people knew I was loaded with cash.

In one of the bases lived a 21-year-old woman named Jaida. Her fella was a little bloke called Micky Drake. He was known to stab people without a second thought and he had a fucking army of back up behind him, so taking his girl seemed like a good idea – what was I thinking? He was dangerous, he was one of Essex's biggest villains and he worked for one of Essex's biggest gangsters, Mark Selby from the infamous "Selby's A127 villains party. Now, these parties were held on the last Saturday of every month and were very high profile among the criminal underworld. People from all over the country would travel for hours upon hours to attend these gatherings. I even spotted a few celebrities on more than one occasion, such as Lenny Henry, and a couple of the gladiators; 'Rhino and Shadow' were also seen there by myself (and no, I was not seeing things).

I soon became a regular face at these parties and mixed with Essex's big boys. This was a mansion with an indoor swimming pool and a massive out barn with a bar in, sofas in a chill-out room and a DJ stand at one end for all to party in sounds all nice right? Wrong, This place was grimy!. This was a lot of fun at the time but was the messiest place I had ever been, people were overdosing on a regular basis from bad pills or trips and a lot of the time just left outside literally in the gutter with a bottle of water to get through it alone whatever the outcome. Live or die. Quite a few people died at those parties along with a lot of lives ruined from people fucking up their heads with huge amounts of mind-bending class A drugs, including me.

The police had tried stopping these parties for years. I'm sure 'Selby' was paying them off. It even came out that 'Selby' had a pill pressing machine and was making his own ecstasy tablets, so fuck knows what was going into them. He was also using a bottle sealing machine for Evian water, taking it straight out of the tap. Fucking hell, it's like only fools and horses all over again, ha. The swimming pool was known for its use by the crack heads (mainly black fellas). It's a known fact that the hit from crack smoke hits you the very instant you blow it out and the longer you hold it in, the stronger the hit. These fellas used to sit on the side of the pool in their boxer shorts and suck in a massive pipe, then they would swim as many lengths underwater holding their breath as much as they could before coming up and blowing out the smoke for the rush… There were some fucking sights in there I'm telling ya.

Then there was the main barn, this had one well-lit area with a bar and loud music, and this was where the white people mainly would stay. Then you had the dark end of the barn with no lighting and the sound coming from the 'DJ' playing in there was deafening but I loved it and even though it was looked upon as taboo for a white boy to enter the area, I found myself up there a lot, really just to prove to everyone I didn't give a fuck even though I could have been stabbed in the dark and tossed outside quite easily, and believe me it was threatened on more than one occasion. I was regularly flashed knives and guns from under peoples jackets or waistbands this happened at least four times up that end as if to say, "Fuck off, back up the other end, little white boy."

I fucking didn't. One night, I asked a young white fella in a suit up the light end for some coke as I could see him serving up other people, he said, "Yeah, no problem," and passed me a wrap of white powder for £50 – I know my drugs. I opened this powder and clocked it was not right straight away just by looking at it. I sniffed a line and it burnt my nose like crazy, it was a £5 wrap of CUT SPEED. I was not fucking happy to say the least. I jumped up out of my seat in a rage and went to pull this young fella and as I put my hand on his shoulder somebody grabbed my arm, an old grey-haired bloke and said to me, "Leave it, son. They are the Richardson's nephews, they'll have you killed, my boy. There's a good lad, run along." They had just mugged me off for £45. I wanted to gas the prick and glass him, but to this day, I'm glad I left it or I might not be here now. There was two of them and they looked like brothers. I'm sure they thought that they were their uncle's, both suited and booted. The Richardson's were the Krays rivals back in the day, so… Sensibly I left it alone.

Me and my pal, Timmy spotted Rhino from the gladiator's show, he was a fucking lump and a half. Timmy and I were trying to decide if his size was made of water retention and fat or solid muscle. So…I decided to find out. I walked straight up to him and said, "Alright fella," and I poked him hard in the abdomen, my finger crumpled against his rock-hard stomach like a thin plastic straw up against a solid brick wall. He just looked at me in the eye and said, "FUCK OFF" and so I did sharpishly although laughing to myself. I went back to my mate, Timmy, and told him what had just happened and how funny it was, he did his nut and wanted to go and fight with the bloke. It took me ten minutes to calm him and stop him as he would have got done, no doubt. Thinking he's invincible on the drugs, huh don't they all, or don't WE all, hmm?

Mark Selby was a playboy millionaire. He used to walk through the party with a few scantily clad young girls on his arm all pilling out of their faces and waiting for more free drugs that mark kept on him all night to feed people straight out of his top shirt pocket as if he was feeding his herd. He used to walk around just placing pills in certain people's mouths that he knew for free, knowing they'd be back for more later with their CASH OUT. He was quite the celebrity on the night; everybody wanted to talk to him. Not me! I was going to get to his money through the little rats that run for him! He didn't impress me.

I used to go with my best mate Luke and quite a few others of us. The big Q crew we were called. This was not a place like 'Selby's' to go in small numbers, though I had been known to go alone like a fucking loon with a meat cleaver down the back of my trousers for protection, stupidly, but I would always see people I knew in there anyway. After Luke recently clocking that my surname is Slaven, he informed me that I had a few brothers and sisters out there through Brian (my biological father). I thought nothing of this until... So, one night, I'm dancing on ecstasy completely out of my nut and clueless to my surroundings, and this girl approaches me. She looked like the type of girl who liked a fight, like a geezer. She shouted over the music, "Your name Scott?"

I said, "Yeah, what the fuck has it got to do with you?" (coz I'm a charmer like that)

She said, "I'm your sister! My name's Loulou, we've got the same dad!"

Now for any normal person, this would affect them in a completely different way but I just said, "Alright sis, fancy a pill or three?"

I could see she was fucking nutted too her jaw was swinging all over the place.

She said, "Fuck yeah, you got some?"

So I gave her two out of my shirt pocket; she took my beer and necked the pills together. I don't really remember the party that night but I did show my new sister that I had some bollox and that I didn't give a fuck for danger. I said to her, "Come with me," and I took her up to 'the dark end'. It was where all the black fellas hung out and where the DJs were playing from, but white people were not welcome up there. I wanted to show EVERYONE I didn't give a fuck and NOTHING would scare me 'I can't even explain why I felt the need to do this! I was just young and 'fucking stupid''. On more than one occasion, I had guns pulled on me in the area and told to leave. I didn't.

"Fucking shoot me! Is it worth the aggravation of having to get rid of me? What, because I'm dancing where you dance? C'mon, for fuck's sake." I was lucky!

Oh, one thing I do remember of that night was the walk home with my pals and my newly found sister at around five in the morning. We had all been on our different cocktails of drugs through the night so theoretically we would all be seeing different things but Loulou and I came just passed Holy Cross Church and we grabbed a hold of each other in panic. As we looked down the road, we could see a lynch mob heading our way with lit torches and machetes etc. We shit ourselves, and because we were both seeing the same thing at the same time, we were totally convinced that we were right and the others were lying to us to stitch us up and lead us into our death or something. We refused to walk any further as the mob didn't seem to be moving towards us, just staying still waiting so we hugged each other and planned another route. But the only way was across the even darker fields and through a cemetery which out of your box (on hallucinogenic drugs) is not a good idea. After half hour of persuasion by all my pals, we discovered it was just bushes and lamp posts. Nuts, right? This was my first experience with my sister and it wouldn't be the last fucked up time we'd have together either.

The last Saturday of the month rolled around again and we all started getting tooled up and getting our drugs ready to sell at Selby's. The evening approached and we left Laindon to go to the infamous party. We approached the party coming down the A127 in a car for a change as opposed to walking and the place was lit up from a mile away, only this lighting was BLUE! We pulled off the main road and on to the massive long driveway, as soon as we pulled up we see old bill everywhere swamping the place. There were even two helicopters with armed police dangling from rope ladders ready to drop into the gardens of the party (as it just backed onto fields) and shut it down. Would this spell the end of these gatherings of hardcore criminals?

As you can imagine, we didn't hang about. I told Mark (the driver) to spin around and get the fuck out of there sharpish as the car, with us in it, was packed full of class 'A' drugs. We all would have got years inside. Well, I wouldn't because I would have dropped the drugs I had in the car and blamed the driver as he was a right fucking idiot anyway. He was not a mate. He was a plum and just 'the driver'.

I used to wait for Micky Drake to get out from his and his bird's flat and I'd use Jaida's place as a base for the evening. I told her I was 18 (I was 14) it wasn't long before she came on to me and so did her sister. I had a choice to make, did I get with the sister and have no complications or take Jaida from Micky Drake 'the nutter' and face a possible stabbing? huh, what do you think I did? That's right I started to see Jaida behind Micky's back of course. After a period of time, I heard Micky had caught wind of something going on between me and Jaida and he put the message out that he was going to stab me. No way was I hiding away from my playground because of him. I didn't give a fuck. I walked to cranes court and who did I see from a distance? Micky Drake – shit, here we go…
I just went into psycho mode and I screamed at Micky, "ere Drake, you little cunt, you pull a knife on me you better be

fucking quick with it or I'll take it off you and fucking carve you up with your own tool you MUG!"

He approached me with a black fella and a big white bloke on either side of him (his muscle/protection) he put his hand out to shake my hand laughing and said to me, "I've heard all about you and mate, you have got the biggest pair of bollocks of anyone I've ever met, you can have her (meaning Jaida) and good luck making money, I have heard you are good at it."

He offered me pills for 75p each (they sold for ten pounds each at the time). I'd go as far to say a sort of partnership was instantly forming, he wanted me to work with him, he thought I'd be handy I suppose. Little did he know I was a horrible little cunt and I planned to take his business and customers, I had already taken his missus!

75p when you want a thousand pills is a lot of money when you're 14-years-old, huh? £750…bollox I was planning to get them for free somehow. Jaida knew Micky well (obviously), so my first move was to get closer to her. I moved in with her. My mother was not happy, to say the least, but it was a business move in my eyes as Micky remained friends with her. He would tick her anything any time, "touch" so… The first move was to get Jaida to tick 1000 E's off of Micky; this would give me roughly £10,000 more or less to start me off. It didn't quite work out like that way though, I just told Micky he was 'knocked' and I spent the next few weeks getting shit faced on pills. I can't tell you much about that as I don't remember much of it. It got to a point where at one stage I was sat on the bed talking to a little green man in front of everyone. I can still picture it to this day.

He was sat on the edge of the mattresses and his little green legs were dangling; he looked like a miniature space type thing with an antenna on his head, he was like a little cartoon character. I had been awake for four days and I was sat there talking to this little alien type thing for at least an hour. People that were coming and going to the flat to score off of us were being very wary of me as I must have looked like a complete schizophrenic sitting there talking to thin air, *ha, ironic now!* I didn't do these things to scare people into thinking I was nuts, I genuinely hallucinated on a regular basis and thought nothing of it, in fact, I fucking loved it. I even thought it was funny not knowing the damage I was doing to my brain 'long term'. I don't find it funny anymore, for many reasons.

We were on the third floor and one day I was out my nut and there were a few of my mates there, all of a sudden I got up and walked over to the window and said, "What? Yeah, you go down the road chuck a left, keep going and it's up on the right!"

Then I sat down without saying a word to anyone. Nobody questioned what had just happened as this sort of thing had become normal. I was killing my brain. After a couple of minutes, I got back up and went back to the window and screamed at the top of my voice, "Well, what the fuck you asking me for then, FUCK OFF YOU MUG!!"

Then I returned to my seat, again saying nothing and acting completely normal. Luke Nevendon plucked up the courage and said to me, "What was that all about, bruv?"

I just said, "Oh, that was just Dave he asked me where the closest McDonalds is, so I told him, and then when I sat down, he called me back to the window and said he didn't want McDonald's anyway, so I told him to fuck off!"

Luke said, "But mate we're on the third floor."

I replied, "Yeah, his name is Aerial Dave, he flies, innit?" Everyone just roared out with laughter, my mate even fell off his chair laughing so hard. I really did talk to somebody floating. Putting the drugs aside for a moment and just taking you slightly off topic, I have a theory. I am a strong believer in the spirit world and afterlife. My theory is that THIS, where we live in, is hell. We are trapped inside a living body that we have to strive to keep alive and generally fear death just to end up watching all our older loved ones pass away one by one and then die ourselves to leave our younger loved ones devastated and distraught, and that's only if we are LUCKY and don't die early from an illness or an accident or even being killed by some fucking nut job. But once we pass with the secret that 'it's a better world as a spirit', we are just forever waiting for all our loved ones to join us one by one, never to be parted again, as free spirits, never a pain again, able to visit the entire world freely; think about it. No illnesses, no pain, no need for money or food etc, etc, almost as if you are in an endless dream. No fear or even possibility of death, it seems obvious to me. Yet not obvious enough for me to take my own life and find out, though I have attempted to take my own life twice and I have been clinically dead and resuscitated once, ironic really…

I heard something on a TV show years and years ago that was apparently from a play called 'Wee Chlo' (or, as some people call it, *Huit Clos*) and it stuck with me. It said… *The torture and the torment is other people, that's what hell is, other people, slowly driving each other mad all wanting things they can't have, all tearing each other to pieces with the destructive power from their unsatisfied desires, but unable to escape from each other because of the terrible chains of power and love and sex and guilt and money that bind us all together!*

Not exactly how I would put it but bloody close. Now, I was about to take a step up the ladder, well, I was going to jump up it once again without even knowing it. Jaida knew a big bloke named Dale Martinez. Every time I saw him he was with two other blokes named Jack and Shay. Jack was quite a lump, quite stocky white fella, very laid-back type whereas Shay was a black comedian, the geezer was normally dressed in some outrageous outfit of some luminous colour (a green jumpsuit). I remember well, he was always just bouncing off the walls with energy (out of his nut), ha. I had heard this bloke, Dale's name a few times when some big deals were being done in quite a few different bases so he must have been one of the top dogs. Well, how lucky that Dale took an instant liking to me (as all dealers seemed to) and after spending only a couple of hours with me he wanted me on the payroll. He thought I was 'fucking bananas'.

Now a couple of weeks passed and this Dale was on the scene almost every day all of a sudden. He was grooming me, and flashing his cash knowing what he was doing as he could see and hear that I was hungry for it. He knew I could be a weapon and to him, completely disposable too, though I couldn't see it at the time. As time went on and Dale was round Jaida's a lot to see me (or so I thought), I got to see that people really feared this bloke. He was a big lump well over 6ft and just as fucking wide. I mean, this cunt could just about fit through a doorway but you know what? He didn't intimidate me in the slightest, and I think that's what he liked and what made him think that I was good to have around, especially when it comes to collecting money or scaring people. *Pay or your door comes off its fucking hinges and there's some 5ft 8 crazy cunt wielding a gun or a knife threatening to kill you all and douse you in petrol,* I think you would pay up. And he knew this. He grew to love me it seemed, he even used to grab me and kiss me on the forehead every time he saw me. This geezer was fucking crazy in the head. He used to cuddle up to a different samurai sword every day of the week and not just for protection, oh no, this bloke said that he was in love with them. Hmmm, strange one, I know.

Jack and Shay were a couple of fucking nutters too. The nicest two blokes you could wish to meet though, you would just want them in the tent spitting out and not outside the tent spitting in if you know what I mean?! They used to make their money ram-raiding off licences around London for the fags and expensive booze. They used to just reverse into the shop front while it was closed late at night and two of them would jump out and fill the car whilst Jack (the driver) stayed in the car ready to fuck off double-quick. Some nights they would do five shops. They were earning well from it but it was obviously not consistent, whereas what they were doing with Dale was, and it was bigger money. Yeah it carried a higher sentence if you were caught, but there was less chance of being caught if you knew the right people and was good at keeping secrets, and all of a sudden, I did and I was.

We were about to have the same set up as 'the Essex boys'. VIP access and a licence to sell drugs at extortionate prices for massive profits inside the clubs of Essex and

Stratford. We were probably making more money than the bar most nights. Certainly more profit than any bar in any club we went into on any one night, that's for fucking sure!

I had three bosses as I said, and these bosses were working the clubs exactly the same as Pat Tate and Tony Tucker were, only to this day they are not known because they haven't been killed or nicked, hmm seems all wrong to me, But definitely strange. Oh well, could it be that we were cleverer? More careful? Or just not as big in the game yet?

To make the money we made, be unknown and still be alive? I think we, (well, they) did fucking well. So, as you now know my bosses names were Dale, Jack and Shay. These fellas were working a few clubs selling E's and pure speed (amphetamine) how much they were making I still have no idea because I don't know how many of them there were working for them like me. They wanted me to work at two clubs. Space in Stratford and Palace hotel, Southend. I never knew what club I would be at the next coming weekend. I was told at the last minute, literally an hour before we went when at the same time I would be loaded up with E's and speed. I was NEVER stopped or searched at the doors and I was fucking 15 years old only. I thought I was a fucking gangster. What an Idiot!!! I was a pawn in the game and that was it. Completely disposable!!! I was trusted to keep my mouth shut if I got nicked though and I was also seen as someone not to be fucked with despite my young age, I was told I looked the part too. I was very loud and 'in ya face' all the time which made everyone I met very wary of me and some fucking hated me. Most people I had dealings with would be straight with me with no fucking about like with money etc, in case I kicked off. Only some people knew what I was capable of but I think

61

it came across loud and clear to others anyway. I even used to wear bright white brand-new trainers into a shoes only club as I was working in there. It used to cause an uproar with people seeing me go in whilst getting turned away for the wrong kind of footwear or clothing. Now when I look back, it was really fucking stupid drawing attention to myself like that but back then things in the criminal world were so much easier to get away with, I didn't care. I loved it! I felt like a boss and I didn't give a shit that I was being flashy and obvious. But would that be my downfall? Maybe, maybe not.

I met these three at cranes court, 'the Bronx of Basildon' as I said they used to come to Jaida's, they had all heard of me despite all of them being much older than me and through what they had heard they wanted me on their payroll as I said, 'on the firm' as they called it. I was moving up in the world, or so I thought, but would it last? Would I get rich? Would I end up dead, was also a question I used to ask myself. If I am being completely honest, I still do because of the naughty things I have done throughout my entire life. Have you ever prayed to god though you do not even believe in him? I bet the answer is yes… I know I do nearly every day through sheer anxiety caused by my past actions and things still occurring to this day due to being the way I am. Do yourself a favour and do not follow in my footsteps at this stage of the story, *maybe wait until the end*… unless you want to end up fucked in the head like me. If I hadn't changed the names in this story, I would be being hunted for right now. I would be a dead man as some of the characters are still active criminals to this day. Well, the ones that are not in jail or dead at least.

Ecstasy was massive on the club scene and even more popular with the gay scene, so the bosses thought mixing the two together would turn out to be a fucking huge moneymaker. We heard about the 'Coco Cuba' club/night in the Palace Hotel in Southend which was a gay/transvestite night. I was about to jump up the ranks again. I was told this is how it would go; we would arrive at the club with about a thousand pills (ecstasy). We had paid seven hundred and fifty pounds for these (if we paid for them at all), we were about to take about ten thousand pounds, give or take a few quid, now that's some turn around in two and a half hours. We needed to be looking smart but we would be allowed trainers as long as they were flash and clean. We would enter the club at midnight, the club closed at two-thirty a.m. The first hour I would spend walking around and around the nightclub scouting for other dealers, asking everybody that looked the slightest bit like a dealer.

"Here mate you got any pills?"

My job was to clock and remember who was carrying and report back to the boys, they, in turn, would quietly inform the doorman who was on the side and got their payment too. The doormen then would approach these people and search them, take their drugs to keep for themselves to sell on another night when we weren't there. They then offered these people/dealers the opportunity to leave without their pills and drugs etc, sometimes even cash would be taken depending on how much drugs were being held. People will give up a nights takings to save themselves a nicking (the doormen's payment) and without informing the police. Of course, every single one of them got out as quickly as possible, no questions asked. Within an hour, the club was at least 80% cleared out of dealers and we were more or less the only ones left. I was selling the pills we had paid 75p each for, for 15 quid each or

15 quid for two if I was given the go-ahead or if I felt generous after a few drinks and a few dozen of the pills myself. Two and a half hours saw us take a minimum of 10,000 pounds of cash out of that club. I even sold to a copper one night. A young quite attractive little blonde woman approached me, I could see she was old bill a mile away even though she was gorgeous, I shit myself.

She said to me, "Look, mate, you can ask your bosses, I am a police officer but I am not at work and I want to have some fun, I am safe you can ask them."

I looked over at the boys I was working for and they gave me 'the nod' so I served her up. If I remember right, she took 3 pills. I charged her twenty-five quid and off she went… Fucked up eh? The amount of pills and speed I was taking at 14 years old was ridiculous.

One night, in our two and a half hours in the club, I took fifteen E's and fourteen grams of pure base speed (paste) enough to kill anyone. Half of an ounce of speed and 15 pills. Unbelievable and fucking stupid! I am lucky to be alive. (And I hope anyone reading this wouldn't be so fucking stupid). This scam between the two clubs went on for quite some months too, maybe even a year.

One night, I was travelling back to Basildon from the palace hotel where I'd been working the night selling pills again. The time hit half-past two and it was chucking out time. I was left with about 100 pills roughly so with nobody knowing, I pulled out the driver's ashtray in his car and stuffed the pills behind it. I was also holding seven-eighths of solid cannabis cut and wrapped ready for sale that I'd put in the actual ashtray (I had only sold one). The driver knew about these (the puff only). We got half-way home around about

Leigh-on-sea, and fuck me, the blue lights went on behind us despite the driver driving like Miss Daisy, and we got pulled by the police. They asked us all to get out of the car and stand in a line on the curb of the side of the road, so we did. They asked us if there was anything that shouldn't be in the car as they were going to search it now. I whispered to the driver of the car, "Show them the puff," so he did. The police were happy for the find and immediately stopped searching. I was not really bothered because everything was stashed in the driver's car so he would get the blame without a doubt and as I said before, he was a fucking melt so I wasn't fussed. We just used him to drive us around. The old bill searched us all before starting on the car. We were all placed under arrest for the puff because I wouldn't own up to it (and believe me I was sticking to my story).

We were taken to the closest police station for questioning, which was Westcliff I think, nothing was mentioned about the pills even though we were told they would go over the car thoroughly at the station. Hmmm, anyway, they obviously didn't because the pills were not brought up. So, the first one released was Davey Legg, remember him? (The bully from junior school.) I had a lifelong plan for this boy and it was being put into action slowly but surely. I used him to do anything I said, it was my turn to bully him. I passed him as he was getting released he said to me, "Fisher, I ain't got nowhere to stay."

I said, "Go to Jaida's, tell her I sent you and it's sweet and I'll see you there when I get out."

The morning came and I was released without charge. The driver of the car got 'done' for intent to supply cannabis and given a court date. He even asked me to own up to it. I told him to fucking jog on. Huh 'never mind eh'. I called 'the driver' in the morning and told him to get to me now. 10 minutes later he arrived at Cranes Court, I jumped in his car and pulled the ashtray completely out, the bag of over 100 pills was there. 'The driver' was in shock; he didn't know I'd put them there, he wanted half of them. I told him to fuck off again and got out the car and told him to leave, well, maybe not as politely as that but still. When I first got back to Jaida's in the morning she said she had something to tell me but she was petrified of what my reaction was going to be. It turned out Davey Legg had climbed into bed with Jaida while she was sleeping and tried touching her up. She pretended she was in a deep sleep and just kept batting his hand away again and again until she had to forcefully push him off of her. I fucking flipped. I went and saw my pal, 'Tommy Broomfield'. I was on the hunt for the dirty little cunt.

Tommy said, "I'm after that little shit, he's a grass (police informant) mate and he's just fucking bubbled me up for a burglary that I didn't do. He did it and gave my name!!"

So we went out together to find him, I had a massive kitchen knife and Tommy had his reputation. Tommy was covered in tattoos including all over his face, and head. He looked scary even though he was a tiny little bloke; he was like a fucking Pitbull. We went straight to cranes court knowing he would be there somewhere. After searching for about ten minutes, I found him hiding in an alleyway down a set of steps. He could see by my face that he was in shit in a big way.

I called for Tommy, I grabbed Davey Legg by his hair and I pulled out my 9-inch kitchen knife and I put it in his mouth and screamed at him, "Talk to me, talk to me, I'm gonna cut your fucking tongue out unless you tell me what you fucking did! You filthy little cunt!"

Tommy came flying around the corner and I was bouncing Davey's head off of the top three steps (of about eight) by grabbing him by the hair and slamming him face first into the steps. I threw Legg Davey by his hair at Tommy's feet and Tommy simultaneously kicked him hard in the head like a football. We picked him up; Legg was wearing a west ham scarf. Tommy tied it into his mouth and around the back of his head. I got one end and Tommy got the other and whilst kicking the shit out of him we pulled as hard and tight as we possibly could until the corners of Davey's mouth split. He was literally squealing like a pig being slaughtered. It all happened outside Jaida's front door, so I called her out to let her watch him beg for forgiveness. Then we let this little scummy cunt go. This boy had crossed me all my life. What was my reaction going to be? It was something I thought about for years (as I can be a patient man, he who laughs last, laughs longest yeah?) I would one day ruin Davey Legg's life, FOREVER!

I was gaining quite a reputation for such a young boy. I loved a fight. One evening, I don't remember what cocktail of drugs I had been on, I couldn't possibly remember every time, but I was sort of chilling with Jaida on the three mattresses stacked up as a bed and I was watching some music on TV. All of a sudden I could hear a load of shouting from what sounded like two or three blokes outside. So I jumped up as one of the voices I recognised and he was shouting for help. I remember it was quite odd as the voice I could hear calling for help was my mate, Alby. He was over 6ft tall and a big old lump and must have weighed in at around 20 stone, big skinhead geezer, none the less, I ran outside to see what was going on. When I got out there it was just Alby (who is massive) and this regular-sized bloke on top of him, beating the shit out of him, repeatedly punching him in the face and Alby was calling for help. So I jumped about eight steps and took a run at them. Clyde (the bloke on top) didn't see me coming and I just kicked him square in the face with my full force and he flew off of Alby into the matrix position (horizontal in the air) and landed on his back. As he landed, I said to Alby to fuck off home and get cleaned up. I thought this Clyde bloke was out for the count. I turned my back and walked back up the steps to Jaida's bedsit and then I heard, "Excuse me, mate."

I turned and it was this bloke, Clyde, covered in blood.

I said, "What?"

He replied, "Can I ask you your name?"

I said, "You can ask me what the fuck you like, you cunt, but you won't always get the answer you might want!"

He approached me. I was on about the third step, I think, and he came running at me with a flying kick. So I simply grabbed his raised leg and pulled him hard towards me by his foot. As I did, he lost his balance on the raised steps. I then grabbed him by the back of the head and launched him face first into the brick wall directly behind me beyond the top step. I repeatedly smashed his face into the brick wall until he was begging me to stop. The blood was everywhere and then Jaida came running out and jumped on his back whilst I had a hold of him, punching him in the face and rib cage. She pulled his expensive leather jacket off him and took it into hers as I threw him down the steps in a state and told him to fuck off.

He said, "I'll be back," as he stumbled off so I shouted at him, "Who the fuck are you? Arnie ya cunt! You best bring a fucking army or a gun, you mug or you'll get done again... PRAT!"

That was the last I heard from him but I did hear that he was telling his friends that I was one hard bastard and he wouldn't want to fight me again. Job well done I would say.

I was still selling anything that came up cheap (pills, speed, clothes, anything). I decided to stop getting high on my own supply and go sober for as long as I could, which turned out to be about a week, I think. I'm not sure it was a good idea to suddenly stop everything at once though because one night during time I climbed onto the three mattresses Jaida and I had on the floor for a bed. She went straight to sleep with her back to me sort of which was odd because she was a nymphomaniac and wanted sex EVERY night, so why not tonight? Was she pretending to sleep? I had been with her for about six months and to me, this was different behaviour to normal, or was it me? All I know is I was laying there and I was watching the cover moving over her private parts, (her breast to start off) plus the bed was just a little away from the wall which it had never been before so I thought someone was down there touching her whilst she lay next to me just solely to mug me off in a big way, and bearing in mind I was stone-cold sober at the time. She was into big black men before Micky Drake and I laid there and continued to watch the covers move vigorously around her crotch area for about twenty minutes, all of a sudden I flipped, I lost control. I grabbed Jaida by her hair and literally dragged her to the front door kicking and screaming at the top of her voice with nobody listening, then I picked her up off the floor by her neck and screamed at her, "Get that fucking cunt out from next to the bed or I swear I'm going to carve the cunt up and make you watch and then I'll kill you, you fucking slag. I swear bitch, DO IT!"

She looked at me and nervously laughed and said, "Are you losing the plot?"

Because she laughed at me, I slapped her with the back of my hand and knocked her clean off of her feet, I then proceeded to drag her back up against the wall and screamed abuse at her. I said to her, "You have got someone in there in front of my very eyes and you are telling me there's no one there? All just to make me think I'm losing it you fucking slaggy little cunt!!I know your fucking game."

She was WELL shaken up by now, she said to me, "Well show me then?"

So I grabbed her by the hair again and pulled her back into the bedsit, she had curtains that were from the ceiling to about a foot from the floor, as we fell all over the place going back indoors, I was pointing and screaming at the top of my voice "LOOK, LOOK! behind the curtain, there's his feet. He's trying to get to the open window to get out, FUCKING LOOK!"

Again I was shouting the same thing, "You are trying to make me believe there is nobody there when there is, you wrong'n cunt," the feet stopped moving. It was half-past two in the morning and I got on the phone to my mum and was in a hysterical state and explained to her the situation that there was a bloke there and to please come and see it for herself because Jaida was denying it and trying to make me think I'm seeing things. He was there for fucks sake! I could see him.

I don't remember the next ten minutes it took for my mum to get to me at that time in the morning. I probably continued to beat Jaida and her fucking friend around the room, but when my mum arrived, the front door was open and she walked in. I had a massive kitchen knife in each hand and I was slashing this bloke to ribbons and cutting him to pieces as he lay on all fours on the kitchen floor with Jaida trapped in the corner with blood everywhere. As my mum got close I saw the blood splatter from a slash of the blade, across my mum's face like a flick of paint from a brush.

My mum screamed at me, "What on earth are you doing? Scott, you need help! I think you've lost it!"

I said, "Why?"

She said to me, "There's no one there, son!"

I fell to the floor, my brain had broken down! I could see a dead black man and blood everywhere. My mum told me I was to go with her and so I did. This was to be the end of this relationship between me and Jaida. Huh, never mind, NEXT!!!

That's just how I was. This was her way out too, of a drug-fuelled mind-bending violent possessive relationship. We were over, to my mum's delight, just not the best way to end it but everything happens for a reason. I truly believe that. It was about the same time I fell out with Dale Martinez (one of the bosses, who was fucking Jaida behind my back too and gave me chlamydia). I owed him about £330 and I was short £100 but I'd never been late paying before. Dale changed on me, completely switched and acted in a way I'd never seen aimed at me before. He took the £230 and said he would call me tomorrow regarding the £100 outstanding.

I said, "Dale, I'll never get it by tomorrow." *I was on my arse*

He just repeated, "I'll call you tomorrow," aggressively. The next day rolled around, I got a phone call from Dale.

He simply said, "You got my money? Every day it is going to go up £100."

I said, "But Dale…"

He said simply said, "It just went up," and hung up the phone! Another few days passed and I received exactly the same call every day. Going up £100 every call. Dale decided to step up the intimidation by visiting my mother's house and threatening her, telling her he was going to kill me in front of her then murder her too, oh and my dad (which he thought was Colin) My mum was petrified (he was a big bloke). My mum is 5ft 2" and probably weighs about six stone too, she's tiny. As soon as he left after spitting in my mum's face and threatening my nan too, my mum called me on my mobile and said, "I think you better get around here fucking quick. I have just had some fucking animal at my door threatening to kill us all, GET ROUND HERE NOW."

I knew who it was and I was shitting myself, the debt had gone up about five hundred pounds and I didn't have a penny. I ran all the way home to try and sort this out and make sure my family was okay! Me, my mum and Colin had a long chat about what to do and about how potentially dangerous this situation was. My mum said to me, "Scott, there is only one person I can think of that may be able to sort this out."

I said, "Great who?"

My mum said, "Brian… Your father."

I had heard from people that knew him that he was a fucking maniac and an absolute nut job and one of 'the faces' in the Essex underworld as he used to 'run the door', fuck me didn't they all?

Huh, so I didn't really have to think too hard, I said, "Yeah, I'm ready to meet him. I think it's time I need some fucking help with this one!"

So my mum got in touch with Loulou (my half-sister from Brian, the one I met at A127 infamous Selby's parties) From the things I had heard, I was expecting a real east end gangster looking geezer and that's exactly what he was, he was just missing the long black leather jacket. Me and my mum were like cats on hot bricks just waiting for a car to pull up in the darkness out the front. I had never ever met him and my mum hadn't seen him since the day she did a runner with me under her arm as he was attacking her when I was a few months old. It had been fifteen years. We were all anxious, to say the least. A car pulled up as we were staring through the frosted glass of my mum's front porch, two shadows approached the front door, my heart was in my mouth, what would I say? How would I feel? How should I act?

The shadows got closer and there was a knock at the door, shit... It's him! My mum let him and what turned out to be his brother (my uncle) in. I was sat at the kitchen table, he ruffled my hair and calmly said, "How you doing son?"

It was like he hadn't seen me for a couple of hours and everything was completely normal, *What the fuck??*

I didn't know what to say. Luckily I had my mate 'Lukey' with me, as it had turned out me and Luke realised he'd been scoring speed off of Brian for years and knew him well. I thought it good to have him there and it was support for me through this strange time and also a familiar face to Brian giving the impression right away that I am in the same game in a way, or at least trying to be. So we got down to business, Brian asked me who I was having a problem with.

I said, "Dale Martinez."

Brian laughed out loud and just said, "Ah, little Dale, eh? I know that little prick. Ha, this'll be fun."

'little Dale?' I was shocked by this as Dale for one, was massive and two, I looked up at him as a 'big boy gangster' or so I thought. Anyway, Brian asked if I knew where Dale would be at that moment. As it happened, I did!

He was at Basildon hospital with Jaida and a pregnant friend of mine named Lulu; he was in the baby unit somewhere.

Brian said, "Right, let's get up there now."

Brian was a big bloody fella (bigger than Dale) and when we walked out of my mum's to get in the car, it was a tiny little purple Nissan Micra. Brian was hunched over, sat in the passenger seat as his brother, Ricky, drove because Brian is on a lifetime ban, for what I don't know! Me, Colin, Brian and his brother Ricky got in this tiny purple clown car and drove to Basildon hospital. We pulled up outside the baby unit and almost straight away we bumped into Jaida's sister, Bella, standing outside for a smoke. I told Brian she would be with Dale. Brian called her over; he must have wound himself up on the journey there because he was frothing at the mouth by now.

He said to Bella, "Call Dale Martinez out here NOW you cunt!" Bella was shaken and intimidated from the very first interaction with my dad. She knew what I was capable of but who was this man, right?

She said, "I don't have any credit I swear"

Brian must have sensed that she was lying or something because he asked her to just get Dale's number up on her phone and as she did, Brian looked at her smugly and pushed the green button, it rang and connected.

He said, "You lying little cunt."

Dale answered and Brian said, "Dale, it's Scott's dad (Dale thought it was Colin). I'm outside the hospital I'd like a word!" Dale hung up just as we see him peer through the blinds of the second-floor hospital window and the next thing we know, three minutes after, Dale's car goes screeching past us out of the car park. We jumped back into the tiny purple Micra and proceeded to track him down, we did. My uncle was right up Dale's arse in the car flashing his lights and tooting the horn and pointing for Dale to pull over and eventually he did. He must have thought he was about to deal with Colin, I think, as he got out the car as bold as brass and swaggered half-way over towards the car That we were in, standing in between his and ours. Brian looked back at me over his shoulder as Dale got out of his car giving it the big one putting his strut on and Brian just said, "Watch this son."

He climbed out and in an instant, Dale fell to one knee on the floor as if he was about to fucking propose and I could hear him pleading with Brian saying, "Please, please Brian if I'd have known he was anything to do with you, I never would have given him a thing, I swear, please."

I'd never seen Dale scared and believe me he fucking shit himself. Ha, I loved it. Brian chucked him £100 that my mum had paid and said, "Look, he is my son; now, there is the money Scott ACTUALLY owes you and you can come to me for the rest, right? Now get up off the fucking floor you look like a right cunt! Get up and fuck off before I smash your face in you silly little mug!"

Dale practically got up and ran back to his car and drove off shaken and confused. My uncle and Brian dropped me and Colin home to my mum's. I took Brian's number and arranged to meet him again. Later that night, emotions were running high, to say the least, me and my mum were arguing in a big way. I don't remember what about but Colin decided to back my mum and shouted at me to stop talking and shouting at her the way I was. I told him to stay the fuck out of it. Colin and I ended up arguing which spilled out onto the doorstep. Colin came running at me and pushed me backwards through a bush landing on top of me facing me with my back to the ground. As we wrestled back and forth, Luke (my best mate) came and kicked Colin in the head to get him off of me. I instantly jumped up and give Colin a few kicks in the head too. As I walked off saying to Colin, "You wait, my real old man will fucking bury you."

Colin replied, "Why don't you come back and do it yourself you little cunt?"

Still, to this day, if I'm going to 'lose it' I get a look in my eye. A look Luke Nevendon had grown to recognise and instantly fear (my close family and friends still fear it now). I turned as Colin said that and I gave him the look. Luke took one look at me and just started shouting, "NO, NO, Scott, don't do it!"

It was too late, the black (not red) mist had descended. I turned and ran at Colin who was stood just inside my mum's front door with my little mum in front of him then I also had Luke in front of me waving his arms telling me 'no' but I just waited for a few seconds until I spotted the perfect opening and threw a punch, this one punch broke my stepdad's nose, blacked both eyes instantly and also knocked his tooth clean out. My mum said that that was it between us as Colin was bent in two, moaning in pain from his tooth being knocked out and his nose being split, there was quite a bit of blood. So I walked off with Luke to his house, we were planning on going to A127 party that night, my mum had chosen Colin over me because I punched him. I was at Nevendon's house for about 20 minutes before I got a call to come home and sort this mess out. I thought my mother had chosen Colin over me but when I got home for the chat it was made clear that was not the case at all. Colin asked to go to my room to talk alone so we did. Colin said to me that my mum had made it crystal clear that if she had to choose between me and him it would be me every time, no question and he would have to go. This made me realise my mum really cared for me (because at that age and being on drugs, you don't see it).

He also offered to lend me his new leather box jacket to go to the party in as he'd ruined mine by throwing me through a bush earlier. He also gave me his last three cans of beer from the cupboard and asked if we could forget about it and move on. His last 3 cans. Now if you knew him, you would know what that means. Ha-ha, I think I'd proved my point though I was no little boy anymore!

Even my mums next-door neighbour was another case of a bloke thinking I was just a boy, he was a fucking huge bloke and one day I was out the front arguing with my girlfriend at the time (this was some time later) 'Carisa', it was about 4 o'clock in the afternoon on a blazing hot sunny day and this fella who lodged next door to my mum's house, opened his front door and he shouted at me, "Fucking keep it down, I'm working nights, I was asleep, you little cunts."

So I said to him (in a rage), "The best thing you can do mate is turn around and go back upstairs before I fucking put you back to sleep!"

He screamed, "Right,"

He put on a pair of steel toecap boots and fucking came running at me like an animal gunning for its prey. I was right by my mum's front door and he grabbed me around the neck and lifted me clean off the floor. I mean I was about a foot off of the floor. I thought, *Shit, I'm going to get done here!* So, I hit him, bang in the middle of his chest in the solar plexus with an open palm and it took the wind out of him instantly. As he was winded he took a step back and as he did, I saw my opening and I punched him on the chin as hard as I possibly could. He went down like a sack of shit. I jumped on top of him and repeatedly punched him in the head, face and the body as Carisa stood watching and screaming for me to stop. Colin pulled up in the van coming home from work and saw me on top of this bloke beating him to a bloody pulp. It took Colin about fifteen minutes to get me off of this fella and try to calm me down. 15 minutes is a bloody long time to be getting beaten for. You can do A LOT of damage in that amount of time believe me. I was drooling at the mouth as I was still screaming at this fella who was now pleading for me to stop. He was telling me I had 'beaten him' and that he was 'sorry for starting'. I just told him he was lucky I didn't kill him.

Later that day, Colin and my mum were in the garden doing a bit of gardening and the bloke who owned the house (who also hated his lodger) said over the fence to Colin, "Col, you done a number on the lodger, didn't ya? I couldn't even recognise him."

Colin replied, "It wasn't me mate...that was Scott!" Apparently, the giant lodger had just said that 'the bloke next door did it', he didn't want to admit it was a 15-year-old boy.

So, some time passed and I arranged with Brian over the phone to go round to his house and meet him properly and his wife, Loraine and their young son, who was about two or three years old, I think (my brother obviously). I asked Lukey if he could come with me as I didn't say it at risk of offending or looking soft but I felt safer with him with me as I didn't have a clue what I was walking into and Luke already knew him quite well. Brian agreed it was ok for my best pal to come with me as he knew him and therefore would allow him in his house. I remember he said to come in a few days when he would have his benefit money and could have a drink with me (this, a fella who was once a gangster but was pushed aside because of his mental health; people thought he was a liability as no one ever knew what his next move would be at any given time). I now know he is the next step up from being a schizophrenic. He is a psychopath on paper and in the eyes of the mental health hospitals and prisons. My mate, Luke Nevendon, would not stop warning me in the days leading up to the meeting, as I was known to be very loud and in people's face. I was told time and time again to NOT be like that around him, son or no son. Because he could switch on me as quick as he could switch on anybody (I am being told).

So anyway, yeah, I'm nervous when the day rolled around to go to his house. He lived on the Alcatraz estate in Laindon before it was all knocked down due to it being riddled with drugs. (Quite an apt name for a place for Brian to live being called Alcatraz)

Mainly heroin and crack were creeping in, I was staying well away from all that. So Luke and I walked around there. It took about half an hour to get there from where we lived. All the time the anxiety and knots in my stomach are building almost like butterflies on a first date. What do I call him? Dad? Brian? Will either of those offend him? My dad, being the way he was,, he was often very touchy about many things so already I am walking on a knife-edge before I even get through the door. As I knock, I take a step back and cross my arms in front of me, a sign of defence. I felt very on edge as I entered. I walked in and Brian (my dad) said, "Take a seat son, I've been waiting for this for years. I can finally have a joint with my boy! You do know you are the 'missing link', don't ya?"

I said, "What do you mean 'missing link'?"

He said, "I've been waiting for you to get in touch for years and now that you're here, we can start the business properly." But what was he going on about? He was clearly sober from alcohol but seemed a bit dozy, a bit drunk almost, which now I know was caused by the medication he was on.

Anyway, we sat down and each rolled a joint. There was a lot of prison talk, as the 35 years I've been alive he has probably only been OUT of jail for about 10 of it. Also just a lot of big man talk like – who do you know? Who have you beaten up? All just shit you don't expect to hear meeting your dad properly for the first time. After a while, Brian's wife came in and I was introduced to her and she seemed like a very lovely lady, very timid and shy but maybe there was a reason for that. Because what would the alternative bring on?

We had been there a while and I had clocked, on my way to the toilet, a big stack of 1kg bars of solid cannabis on top of each other on the kitchen side (worth thousands) just from what I quickly eye spied. I didn't say anything about it all though. After a little while longer, a little boy about three years old came down the stairs holding on to the bannister, the tiny little tyke. He had a massive black eye and immediately I switched and said, "What the fuck happened there? Sorry for swearing!"

Brian gave me the look of death I had been told about by my mother and my best mate who had both seen it before, before something bad happened usually, (in me AND Brian) he just starred and said, "He fell down the stairs," and continued to GLARE at me. I went to say something else and Lukey grabbed my arm and said under his breath, "Fucking leave it bruv, leave it, please!"

So I looked at Brian and said, "Oh right."

I turned to the little boy and said, "Shit, that must have hurt little man, eh?"

I don't remember if he even spoke to me (the boy) but I wasn't there long and before I left I said, "Here dad, can you hook us up with some puff to start us up again please?"

He said, "Yeah," then he handed a big lump over along with quite a large amount of speed and told me WHAT I OWED HIM! He said it was on Nevendon's head but still...to charge me after never ever even putting food in my belly for fifteen years of my life! More front than fucking Southend. Shit...huh. Anyway, I sold it, smoked it and sniffed the lot. I didn't see Brian again for a very, very long time. Would I ever see him again? We'll see. What would your advice be?

So, in the last year or so I had made a fortune and spent that same fortune. Had I peaked? I wouldn't say I was bored with the buzz of the pills and speed because it was a different buzz with every pill, and I certainly wasn't looking for anything else but what did my life journey have in store for me? I had a good friend who lived at Cranes Court (my base). His name was Danny Rawley, it was him that eventually ended up in prison for manslaughter because the bloke he stabbed in the arse, died. This would spell the end of the road for everyone at Cranes Court. The 'old bill' were now flooding the place daily, kicking people out and slamming metal doors on so no one could ever get back in these bedsits. Anyway, It was a crack deal gone wrong with a black fella from Tottenham in London. I don't know the ins and outs of it all; I wasn't there, all I know is that it all kicked off in early hours of the morning. I know this because Tommy Broomfield left mine and Jaida's to go to Danny's and he came back and said, "Fuck that, it's all kicking off over there I'm staying out the way."

The next day, I look out of my kitchen window first thing in the morning making a cup of coffee and the forensic team were combing the area on their hands and knees outside ours looking for the murder weapon, which they found. The bloke from Tottenham tried jumping out of the ground floor window with the gear and the money I believe and Danny stabbed him up the arse and unfortunately hit the main artery causing the bloke to bleed to death, quite rapidly I should think. So, apparently, they got the injured dying bloke into a car and drove him back to London thinking the old bill would think it happened there but there was just far too much damming evidence as the murder weapon had been dumped in the

82

bushes out the front of Cranes Court covered in blood still. The car wasn't torched either; it was sitting for the old bill to find full of the victim's blood. Half way through his sentence for the manslaughter, I got told that something went wrong inside and he had to stay even longer than his 14-year sentence. Before he went away, he sold crack cocaine and heroin. I had tried the crack with him by smoking it on a mini Martel bottle fashioned into a pipe by smashing out the bottom of the bottle and placing a wire mesh in the top to burn the crack on whilst sucking on the bottom hole, the buzz was absolutely fucking amazing. Almost similar to the release of sex, I swear, but like the climax of sex for a man, it's over in literally seconds and instead of feeling relaxed and euphoric you just need more and more. You can spend a grand (£1000) a night just for your first time, easy. I had done. Danny told me if he EVER EVER caught me or heard I was doing heroin he would fucking slap me, and he was a hard bastard.

"I wouldn't touch heroin anyway for love nor money; it comes in needles!"

"FUCK THAT!!!"

So, how did I meet Carisa? Well, I was going out with a girl named Alison. I was 15 years old and yes, we were underage as she was 14 years old but both of us looked and acted a lot older than we actually were. I suppose it rubs off from hanging around with older people every day of your life. One day I called Alison and offered to take her out clubbing. Again, yes, we were underage but I knew people on the doors so I would get in and not even get searched. I was basically allowed to play in a club called 'Monroe's' and do as I fucking pleased. This was where we would be going that night. (I will get to Carisa)

Alison said, "Can I come to yours and get ready tonight?"
I said, "Yeah, of course."

I was really looking forward to the night out and our date. I had butterflies and felt really nervous, as I remember, and keep in mind, I was only a kid. I think that feeling gets lost in us as we get older. A date doesn't get me like that now. The day seemed to go on forever waiting for her to come round to my mum's. She called and said she couldn't get to me; her dad had gone out and so she had no lift. I told her to jump in a taxi and I would pay at my end. So, she did! Alison turned up in an old tracksuit, her hair up and messy and no makeup on and really didn't look how I remembered her all done up. I was deflated, if I'm being honest. I thought, *Oh, what have I done?* Ha.

I think my mum was out but I had asked her if this was okay. As soon as Alison turned up we had a large vodka and coke and I popped a pill (ecstasy) without her knowing. I had to 'feel the ground' with her and see if she was into drugs or against them. We went to my room which was joined to a large hairdressing room full of mirrors, ideal to get ready to go out in as I was worse than a fucking woman. I turned the music on extra loud (and my stereo was bloody loud) the neighbours two doors away used to knock and politely ask if I could possibly please turn it down. I generally would, but I had been known to hang out the window and tell them to fuck off too (depending on my mood).

So the music was pumping, the drinks were flowing and without Alison knowing I was 'coming up' on a pill. Everything just seemed the bollox (brilliant). It was a good day to be alive. Alison asked if I would go into the other room while she got dressed as this was our first date. So we were getting ready to go to Monroe's. By the time this girl had gotten ready, which took about an hour, she was absolutely stunning. I was so looking forward to the night even more so now as I was going out with a stunner on my arm. Everyone would be looking at this pretty young girl in the shortest mini skirt you have ever seen. All in black. I was dressed in trousers, shoes (for a change) and a shirt with cufflinks (proper smart). We had quite a few more drinks at my mum's house and then we called a taxi to the club. I was topping up on my buzz from the pill with dabs of pure base speed here and there whilst getting ready. I was as high as a fucking kite and ready to take on the world. I think my jaw arrived at the club about five minutes before me. Ha! Anyone who's ever taken Ecstasy will know what I mean. It's an inside joke. We got to Monroe's and as I had predicted, I knew the doorman who were working that night so I wouldn't be searched. This was a good thing as I had a pocket full of pills to sell and a bag of pure speed for myself and if I hadn't of known the doormen I wouldn't have chanced it. As Alison got more drunk, I started to bring up the conversation about drugs etc, to see where she stood on it. She seemed to be pretty liberal about it all, so, happy days! I said to her that I had some speed left but I went on to explain that this wasn't your ordinary 'cut speed', this was 'pure' and fucking dangerous stuff. She said, "Yeah, yeah, I've done it all before."

I repeated myself as I knew exactly how strong this stuff was. She was adamant she knew what she was doing, so I gave her a half of a gram, which is not a lot if it has been cut but this hadn't at all. I knew she would feel a buzz from it but I was not expecting what was coming soon. Anyway, Alison and I were standing at the bar drinking and shouting to each other over the music when the barmaid who must have been in her 30s came over to us and proceeded to (what I would call) flirt with us. This was shocking; I was 15 years of age and Alison was 14. I was completely off my nut on the pills and speed I had taken freely in with us. I was finding the fact that a woman twice my age fancying me was mad, but the thing is she didn't just fancy me…she fancied Alison too. She was asking us if we wanted to BOTH go home with her as she was single and said we were a stunning couple. Still, I think this was a bit much, and that's coming from me. If only the woman knew how old we were I wonder if she would have acted a bit different maybe. Ha, I reckon so as what she wanted would have been illegal, as in 'sex with TWO minors' and mud like that, sticks. So, the night went on and after about an hour at the bar, we moved onto the dancefloor for a dance, as ya do. We were dancing for about ten minutes and I could feel the effects of the drugs I had taken really starting to kick in strong as the music just takes over you, even more so now as we were dancing and the blood was rushing around our bodies and to our heads. If I am being honest, a few brief moments passed where I thought I was going to lose control and 'fuck up' (overdose) on the pills and speed I had done. I started to grow concerned for Alison. She had only taken half of a gram of speed but I didn't know her background or anything much about her before this night. Another twenty minutes passed and I lost track of Alison on the crowded dancefloor, again, just 'as ya do' nothing unusual about that but after about half an hour of doing a circuit of the club, I still couldn't find her. I noticed a few people crowding around the outside of the 'ladies' toilets. Now, it's normally the 'gents' toilets if there is any trouble, (well at least, it used to be) so I went over. I heard that some girl was overdosing in the cubicle. I shoved my way through the crowd of girls, blokes and doormen right to the front. One bloke grabbed me and said to me, "No blokes in here mate."

I grabbed hold of him and said, "Look at me you cunt, I ain't fucking going anywhere now fucking get out my face!" and he let me go. I got into the cubicle and Alison was slumped over the toilet a pale shade of green and unconscious and covered in sick also her mobile phone was in the toilet. This was fucking worrying, to say the least. A million things run through your head like… Can I bring her back? If she dies will people want me dead? How will her poor family feel? will I go to jail? FUCK! WHAT HAVE I DONE? Is she going to make it? I did the usual thing you see in a film if someone is dying, you know slap them around the face and shake them about a bit. All of a sudden she started to choke and sort of cough and gargle. Now, this is bad, right? No, this is good. There is life in her. So I picked her up off the floor and did the Heimlich manoeuvre on her and hit her on the back to clear the sick she was choking on. This aided her in being able to breathe again properly. The doormen and I took her straight outside and I told her quietly in her ear on the way out that she had just overdosed and please not to say anything about the speed I had given her. I swore on all I loved I would see her through this and sort her out. I got her to the curb outside the club and sat her down. The news of the near-fatal OD must have sobered her up pretty sharpish because after five minutes, thankfully, she had made a full recovery and she was talking to me completely normally (apart from being pissed). So I took her back to my mum's house where we were staying for the night. I had to walk her around her mate, Carisa's, in the morning for her dad to pick her up as her parents thought she was staying there the night. To be honest, I had wondered how she had been allowed to stay with me considering we were both underage to sleep, well, to have sex together, which I might add we didn't, though I did want to. I could see, blatantly, that Alison was in no fit state to consent to it and I wouldn't do it any other way, so I cuddled up to her for the night. Alison and I continued to see each other and a few weeks passed. Then one day, I clocked Alison's surname was Gray, the same as my nan's maiden name, huh, strange. Yeah, well, stranger than you might think as when we looked into it we found out that we were related. As her dad was my nan's cousin or something like that I believe it was. When Alison found out she came to my mum's house and came up the garden path in floods of tears, I opened the door to her and she was saying, "Oh my god, I think we are related we can't be together can we?"

We asked my mum if this mattered as it was a very distant relation. She told us this was fine so we continued to date and meet up daily. One afternoon, Alison and I met up and decided we would go around to some boys' house where they would be 'having a smoke'(weed). We had been together for a few weeks only I think. I don't remember much detail only that I had never been there before and I didn't know anyone there. One of the boys had a ponytail I remember. Anyway, the evening closed in and it got dark. Alison's very best mate turned up at this house to meet her. She was a tiny little thing with short blonde curly hair and massive boobs and a real natural tanned look to her (almost Mediterranean/olive-skinned!) Because she was so small, her breasts looked even bigger on her too. She was the same age as Alison (a year younger than me), and although not my type and the complete opposite of Alison, very attractive and very pretty. Alison introduced me to her best friend as Carisa. I was immediately attracted to her but knew she was well out of bounds being Alison's best mate. So I thought nothing more of it just continued to chat to everyone and generally take over the room as I always did everywhere I went, just being generally loud and in people's faces intimidating them. Almost trying to install some sort of fear into people thinking it was a way of also gaining their respect. Was I wrong? Well, I was going to find out one day. The evening went on and Alison was in and out meeting different friends etc. I stayed at the house and just got as stoned as I possibly could with the fella whose flat it was and his pals plus a few girls and Carisa. Carisa was very quiet but every time I looked at the girl she was staring at me. I thought she had some sort of jealous streak in her as I was moving in on her best mate. Strangely, Carisa didn't follow her best mate 'Alison' every time she left despite Alison going out about ten times, if not more. Every time I went to the toilet, I would come out and Carisa would be waiting outside the door to use the loo, she didn't say anything she just sort of smiled at me and passed me before I could even get through the door, causing us to brush up against each other facing one another. This was getting stranger by the minute!

As the night progressed, we all ran out of fags(cigarettes) but every time I complained of not having a fag to roll a joint, Carisa was waiting until nobody was looking and throwing me one over, despite other people asking her if she had any and her telling them she didn't. Again, strange! Carisa's eyes were like little slit's where she was so stoned and she just spent the whole evening giggling to herself with a very cunning look on her face, almost like she was up to something. I just couldn't work out what it was. She was Alison's closest friend. After a few fags had been passed 'on the quiet', Carisa had clocked that I kept looking over at her but this was only because I could feel her eyes on me. She was Alison's best mate and therefore off limits. Every time I looked at Carisa, she was sitting on the floor. Now she was flashing her knickers at me by separating her legs knowing she only had a little tiny skirt on and I would see. I watched to see if she was doing this with anybody else. She wasn't. Fucking hell, she's coming onto me. Nah, this is just a test I'm sure. So I didn't give her any reaction thinking she would go straight to Alison to tell her, then 'boom' she would have her best mate back to herself and me out of the way. I was getting the hump with Alison being in and out all evening not knowing what she was really doing. Then one time when she was going out, I followed her out. She was about to get in the back of some flash hatchback motor with three boys to go to Tesco's and get some alcohol but there wasn't enough room for me so I said to her she wasn't to get in the car. She told me she could do what she wanted so I said, "Okay, well, you get in that fucking car and were done! Trust me!"

She said, "Yeah, whatever Scott!" and she jumped in the front passenger seat. I went back into the flat ushered away from the situation 'as I was losing my temper' by none other than… Yep, that's right, Carisa! She was saying things like, "Look, she's not worth it. Let her go if that's what she wants, I'm here!" "She obviously doesn't care about ya."

I thought this was very odd but, *Fuck it, if the opportunity arises, I'm going in!*

90

Alison had left in the car with the boys. I was fuming, to say the least but this anger would be short-lived. I went back into the flat with Carisa and I went straight to the toilet/bathroom alone followed by Alison's 'best mate'. When I came out Carisa was waiting and did the same trick of brushing up against me, only this time she grabbed my crotch. We went into the bathroom and closed the door and kissed each other up against the closed door passionately. We then proceeded to have sex up against the door trying desperately to be quiet but the passion was immense. Carisa wanted to be with me officially straight away and said she wanted to tell Alison when she got back from the shop as she thought what Alison had just done to me was outrageously disrespectful towards me and she thought that Alison deserved to be shown up properly. Man, this was absolute madness!

Alison returned with the boys as Carisa and I waited for them outside the front of the flat and as soon as she stepped out of the car, Carisa told her that she thought she was out of order for going and that she didn't deserve me and that from now me and Carisa would be together. Alison didn't take this well and it kicked off big time resulting in the two of them with each other's hair in their hands, tugging and rolling around on the floor screaming at one another. After I separated them, Carisa and I left together with Alison screaming at us the whole way down the street. The lesson here girls is, if you want to mug me off, then look out because I will always laugh last, and he who laughs last, laughs the longest. This was the beginning of a relationship that would result in serious violence, domestics and hard class 'A' drug 'abuse' including the one drug I would NEVER go near, that's right, heroin, and this would go on right to the bitter end! Oh, and yep...more court cases. This is where, a long time later, I would become known locally as 'the son of the devil'.

A funny thing, every time Carisa and I would split up here or there, for a week or a day down the line, a white pimple would appear on the end of her nose and the day we got back together it would simply disappear. Added, together with the way I treated her, she really thought I was evil. Oh, and my mum "is a witch," too according to her. For reasons that will soon become clear, the story could get a little hazy around about here as I don't remember it too well. Dates and times were non-existent for the next five years and here is how it all began...

One rainy day, I was walking across Frypa fields on my way to Craylands as Mark Richie approached me. Was he going to try and bully me and empty my pockets? No! What he was about to do was far worse than that. He was about to take my entire fucking future away in a heartbeat. This was a moment in my life I would never ever forget for all the wrong reasons, and now still to this day as I write this, suffer the serious consequences of this next part of the story, but will I be by the end of writing this? Well... we'll see!

He said to me, "What you up to, bruv?"

I said, "Nothing bruv, just passing."

We had a quick conversation about getting out of our nuts (it's all anybody seemed to ever think about back in them days).

Mark said to me, "Do you want to try some of this?"

I said, "What is it?"

He replied, "Brown, you smoke it."

I'd never heard of it but this drug was about to take me deeper into the underground life that I was already sort of used to. It was about to get a whole lot darker though and my life was to change FOREVER. I asked him what the buzz was like?

He said, "Let's put it this way, if you have any cares in the world you'll literally forget all about them the rest of the day." What harm could it do, it was only a bit of smoke and it was with Mark Richie. He wanted to share something with me instead of robbing me as normal, I had to do this and maybe form a friendship so I would no longer have to dodge him. Coupled with the dangerous life I was living creating stress and causing me to live life looking over my shoulder and full of anxiety as it was, I could do with forgetting about it all for a day. So we went into an abandoned car garage with the doors ripped off. Mark pulled a roll of tinfoil from up his sleeve. He proceeded to tear a large piece into two smaller pieces, one he left and the other he folded into a tube. He asked me to hold the flat piece of foil as he took out a tiny foil wrap containing the smallest amount of 'brown' powder I'd ever seen (don't forget I'd been used to toilet tissues full of powdered speed and massive bags of white powder like cocaine). This wrap contained 0.10gm of powder, a tenner's worth so I was told, nothing in that tiny amount can harm me surely, so I thought. How fucking wrong could I be.

Mark tipped the tiny wrap of powder onto the foil at one end and made a sort of canal on the foil where the powder was. He put the foil tube in his mouth and placed the flame from his lighter under the foil to heat up the 'brown', it instantly turned into a liquid form (known as 'the beetle') and Mark tilted the foil down to let the substance run down all the while chasing the smoke coming from the burning substance. I'd never seen or heard of anything like it. Mark didn't seem that affected by it but after about eight lines apart from the fact that he was itching his bollocks a lot, mumbling a bit and his pupils had turned to pinholes which made him look evil with piercing eyes. A look I would soon inherit. So I thought I'd try a few and see what happened. Mark had to do it for me as I didn't have a clue. I wondered why he was just giving me something and being nice after the years of abuse and torture from him, even down to as a kid if I had new white trainers on, brand new, he would stamp on them to ruin them and then make you jump up and down to see if he could hear any change in your pockets that he could then threaten you for. Anyway, after three lines of smoke I was instantly sick (something I later in life found out every first timer did).

I said, "Fuck that, I don't want no more of that Mark."

Mark said, "You have got to push past the sickness and you'll feel fucking brilliant, bruv. Trust me, mate."

So to my immense mistake, I carried on until I felt something. I felt euphoric and warm all over and tingly in my hands and feet almost as if all my worries and problems were leaving me through my limbs and out of my toes and fingertips. I'd never felt this warm and content before in my life, especially as I was with 'Mark Richie' of all people in an old run-down garage, just the two of us. This drug was amazing and the complete opposite to what I'd been doing for so long (E's and speed). It was a 'downer' as oppose to an 'upper'; I don't remember leaving that garage at all but all I do remember is thinking was my mum going to see that I was on something and how long would it take to wear off so I'd look okay or did I even look fucked, I didn't know. I went home and let myself in with my key and went straight to my room just in case my eyes told a story. My mum didn't seem to see anything different in me, at least not yet. The next day Mark came to my mum's house and threw a stone up at my bedroom window instead of knocking on the door for my mum to see him (every parent knew what he was but just not the extent of it), still he wasn't chancing it. He called up at my window to ask if I had any money.

I said, "Yeah, I'll be out in a sec."

Mark asked me to chuck in a tenner and I was up for it! We went to Craylands to a bloke called 'biker Jay'. He'd sell anything to anyone including school kids, in their uniform too. He was known for selling puff (solid cannabis) mainly but Mark said he sold 'brown' as well. So I waited around the corner and Mark was about five minutes in there and he returned with another tiny little wrap. I later on in life found out that 'biker Jay' used to lace his solid cannabis with heroin and sell it to kids. Then after a few weeks of giving them that he would groom them onto heroin itself! He had to move off of the estate for that as people wanted him dead and he was receiving death threats through his door and petrol through his letterbox. Hmmm I wonder who would have done that? Anyway, we went back to the abandoned garage to do the same as the day before. Without me having a clue that 'groundhog day' was fast approaching, I met up with Mark every day for about two weeks and every day we were getting a tenner's worth of 'brown' and sharing it. We had started doing it in different places like the stairwells of the maisonettes on the Craylands estate, anywhere out of sight and out of the wind so our flames would stay alight to 'run the brown'.

Anyway, a couple of weeks passed and one day I met up with Mark again and we had no money but I did have a watch my nan and grandad bought me abroad. I thought it was a fake 'Breitling wings' watch but it was too big for me when I first got it. I'd only had it back from the jewellers a few days, who made it smaller and valued this watch as a genuine £10,000 item (it wasn't but still). They even called my mum and offered us insurance for it but I said there was no need I would cherish it forever, right? Mark seemed agitated and pale, almost frail which was completely out of character for him. He asked me if I'd lay my watch on to the dealer who owned the kebab shop and sold brown and cocaine out the back of the shop his name was Naz'. Naz' said to Mark that he had until five o'clock the next day to pay to get my watch back otherwise it would be sold. He said he would definitely have the tenner the next day to get my watch back. I thought, *It's only a tenner, I'll get it somehow even if he don't*. So stupidly, I agreed, and we got our 'bag' (tiny tin foil wrap). We were told it had to be paid by five o'clock, so off we went and smoked it together and went to a friend's house to sit and chill out (out of our fucking nuts). As usual, lately I couldn't remember what happened the rest of the day, I was absolutely ruined, not a care in the world though, or at least so I thought. The next day I couldn't get a hold of Mark at all, I was banging on his door and throwing stones at his window, I was calling his phone and getting no answer. Shit... I needed a tenner before five o'clock or my watch is going to be sold. Normally this wouldn't be a problem I'd steal something and sell it or get some pills from somewhere and make a few quid but for some reason, as the morning progressed, I started to feel ill. I had stomach cramps and every step I took, it felt like someone was kicking me in the back of the legs. Everywhere was aching and really hurting; it was flu like symptoms,

96

everything was so much effort. I gave up trying to find Mark and I went to my pal, Danny Rawley's flat (this was obviously just before he actually went away to prison). I was almost bent over in half, the pain was getting more and more intense. I said to Danny, "Bruv, I'm in fucking bits mate. I'm well ill."

He said, "I ain't seen you in weeks, what the fuck you been up to? You look rough bruvva."

I said, "I ain't been up to much. I've been having a smoke with Mark Richie."

Dale said, "That scumbag?" and asked what I'd been smoking,

I said, "Just brown, mate."

Danny gave me a hard backhand across the face and knocked me off my feet. I shouted, "What the fuck was that for?"

He screamed at me, "You fucking idiot! I told you to stay away from heroin!!!"

I was confused, I hadn't touched a needle, I'd never done heroin. Danny proceeded to tell me that 'brown' was another name for heroin and you CAN smoke it. SHIT!!! My world just caved in at that point. I realised I was in massive trouble now but little did I know just how bad it would get. My whole world was about to change and turn my family upside down forever. 'Once a heroin addict always a heroin addict', that's what people say to this day, In 99% of cases, this is true I'd say. My mother had never ever been involved with drugs in any way. She knew something was wrong but she and Colin had no clue what it could be, all they knew that was my behaviour and attitude had changed dramatically. My mum didn't know what to do so she did what I would consider the worst thing anyone can do and she called the police to come round to her house as my mum had found lists on paper of deals I had done, for example, 28 grams = £280(speed) etc...etc... I had been working everything out I'd been selling and earning on paper. Silly mistake to make but I was just a pup really (beginner).

So I was up Cranes Court and I got a call from my mum saying, "You had better get home now. I have the police here to see you, get home now please!"

I was shitting myself but I had to face it I couldn't hide away from it. They knew where to find me anyway so I'd might as well go and face it. It was only a six-minute walk from where I was across the fields home to my mum's but it felt like I was walking into a sentence. *What did they know or even want with me, was I going to get nicked (arrested)?* Fuck! I could do without this right now. I got to my mum's, there were two officers there, a man and a woman. They asked me to sit down. I could see they had all my paperwork in their hand. They asked me what it all meant. I said, "Clearly you can see what it all is."

They said, "Yes we can, look if you tell us who you are working for we'll just forget about this."

I said, "They are pieces of paper with sums on. I haven't committed any crimes and I don't work for anyone, I swear!"

I put on the fake tears as if I was petrified. Don't get me wrong there was fear there but not enough to make me cry but they bought into it. Mate, don't you worry about that I was good, I was clever. I just denied all knowledge of any criminal activities and they had nothing, just a few scraps of paper with numbers on so that was that, they left. But now weeks had passed and my parents knew something bigger was getting a grip of me. So like I said, again, my mum called the fucking police for advice. She told them my actions and moods etc... They straight away said it sounds like heroin. My mum's world must have caved in at that point too. They asked my mum to set me up in some way, my mother refused and just hung up the phone in the sheer hope that they were wrong. A few more weeks passed and my mum grew more and more concerned as she started to see me deteriorate rapidly and lose so much weight so quick so she started to search my bedroom while I was out of my nut asleep (fucked on heroin). My mum found, stashed in one of my shirt pockets hanging up in my wardrobe, some tin foil with black trace marks on it and a tiny foil wrap containing the tiniest amount of brown powder. She still had no idea what it was and neither did Colin (either that or they were just in hopeful denial). So, Colin took it into work the next day before I even knew it was missing. He took it to a friend of his named Les who was a bit naughty himself. He took one look and said, "Col, if your boy is on this his life is over and yours is going to be hell. That's heroin, mate!"

I don't know how Colin broke the news to my mum. I now know she absolutely broke down. She would have no idea how to even approach this problem let alone solve it. All she knew is what she had been told and that was that my life was over. I was a heroin addict. There was a rocky road ahead, would I EVER get clean now?

One day I went round to my mate, Ross' flat. Well, his mum's, 'Rusty' She used to sell all sorts of drugs to us, youngsters. She would sell puff and weed but to all her pals in their late 30's, early 40's and some older, she would deal in pills (ecstasy) and a lot of speed but never heroin. She was blatantly for all to see bang on it herself too, 24 hours a day, every day. Anyway, I went there one day and I walked in dripping wet as it was pissing down with rain outside and Ross' stepdad 'Black Al' was watching something on the TV with the curtains drawn all cosied up on the armchair. He was roaring out with laughter so I popped my head around the corner from the kitchen to the living room and said, "What are you watching, Al?"

He said, "Friends, bruv."

I said to him, "That's a fucking birds programme, ain't it mate?"

He told me to roll myself a fat joint and sit down and watch a bit with him and he challenged me not to laugh. So I said, "Yeah, I'm game, mate," and I did.

I rolled a joint of skunk and sat down to see what all the fuss was about. After 10 minutes, I must have laughed out loud at least ten times. That's a laugh a minute. It was brilliant. I said to Al, "What's this on TV, mate?"

He told me, "no," and that he had a load of them on VHS video but he said that there were loads and loads of episodes and that he only had a fraction of them and he was collecting them. So I thought for a minute. It was the time leading up to Christmas and Woolworth's used to leave their videos in their cases to save time in the rush leading up to the festive holiday. So I told Al to write down all the episodes he was after and I would go to the town armed with the list and get them, as many as I could get away with each time. Yeah that's right, I had gone from taking ten grand a night to stealing poxy video's. Before I could even blink, the orders for Friend's videos were coming in thick and fast and not just from Al and Rusty but all of their pals jumped on it too. I was taking enough over the whole month to keep my new found heroin habit at bay, as it was so easy to walk out of Woolworths with armfuls of stuff, let alone pockets and bags filled with things. Rusty's pals were all paying cash whereas Rusty herself used to pay me in solid cannabis or Thai weed. I must have stolen at the very least, working it out over that month, 350 videos totalling a retail price of about £2,000, if not more, and that was just me for one month or more like only three weeks. By the time I finished, after continuing to thieve these videos until late January, they cottoned on to what was going on and took all the films and videos back out of the cases and put behind the counters again. Al and Rusty had the entire collection. I mean I was walking into the shop picking them up and ticking them off the list as I went, blatantly as I was desperate for my heroin fix so that I wouldn't get ill. One day, I even decided to leave the shop via the front main entrance instead of my favoured rear entrance leading to the multi-story car park. As I was walking out of the doors with my arms full of videos (about ten cases), I walked straight into the most well-known copper in the town. Shit! My heart just sunk to my stomach and I felt sick I thought I had been caught. He just must have thought it was too brazen as he just bent down and helped me pick them up. He stacked them back in my arms and said, "Have a good afternoon."

I said nervously, "Yeah, thanks a lot," and I left sharpish before he twigged. To this day that still baffles me why he did that. I still believe that because I never used to hide things when stealing I would just walk out of wherever with the items in my hand, I was caught a lot less than someone trying to hide something in their pocket or up their top etc. I think that must be the reason for the copper not really clocking it unless he just felt sorry for me which I doubt very much as the police have never took too fondly to me. Had it really come down to this? This was what I would call petty crime but when I look back I'm not so sure. Even when I think back to Rusty and all her pals asking for selection boxes and tubs of quality street etc for Christmas, it was because they were so expensive back then. So my mates and I went to a certain shop where there was an old lady working a certain shift every day. Once we clocked her shifts, we went in and turned the camera one day to scare her into letting us do what we want within reason. We didn't want money out the cash register but what we did want was ALL the boxes of chocolates and selection packs they had on the shelves. So once we had told her the situation and we scared her, every time we would walk in she would turn her back, pretend she was sorting out the cigarettes and let us take the lot, (man things had got bad). We had to leave it for a few days so that they could restock it all then we would just simply come and take it all again and she was letting us until she left for her own safety. Still, the videos were the better earner not that it was a fortune. It really wasn't.

Rusty had a friend named 'Linda' she also sold puff and weed but no 'class As'. She wasn't as hectic as Rusty, Rusty was nuts. One Christmas, I took my presents from underneath the tree at home at my mum's house, unwrapped them and anything worth any money I took straight around to Linda's to sell to her. She used to buy second-hand clothes for fuck's sake, so if you had something brand new and with tags on you could almost guarantee she would buy it for the right price but because she was paying in puff you would generally get a good deal from her. It was quite funny all the clothes I sold to her, her daughter was wearing on boxing day. Ha. Two sizes too big for her and with men's designs. Oh my days, poor kid!

After thieving things for a while it obviously moved on to bigger things (as it always does). All my mates were moving on to burglary from houses and nicking flash cars, whereas I didn't quite go that far but I did get into nicking motorbikes and mopeds (they were a giggle), and breaking into cars and vans for the stereos or tools in the vans. Disgusting really when I look back, that was people's fucking livelihood but, "kids, that's what drugs will do to you and turn you into!" you will beg, steal and borrow to feed the habit. It will be out of your control!

I had one moped out over the fields one sunny day. I used to keep it in my mum's back garden in the metal shed for hiding, I told her I had bought it. It was ideal as you had to ride straight into a bush and through it to my mum's back gates. It was all very well set up for an escape in case the police decided to come over on their bikes to catch us (not that they could ride them properly). It didn't matter that I was on a cub 90 moped, if you know how to ride and you have a route all planned out, you CAN get away! Anyway, it was a lovely sunny afternoon and we decided to get the little moped out for a laugh, if you only rip up the fields for about half an hour its likely nobody will be called, like the police for example. This bike did about 50 mph I reckon, so on a field, it seems a lot quicker. Anyway, my mate Dave Trotter asked me if he could have a go. So I asked him did he know how to ride it as he wasn't part of our regular riding gang, I didn't know. He said, "Yeah, yeah, of course I do mate."

He didn't want to look silly, so he got on and off and he went slowly at first (not that this thing was fast anyway). As he got further away he started to pick up speed to try and 'top it out' (max speed). He turned around and started heading towards the car park that was over by a cricket hut. This car park had a mound of mud all around it. I would say about two feet tall, like a solid boundary. Dave was heading straight for it at top speed and was shouting to us, "Where are the breaks?" and he repeated this time and time again and we were all shouting back at him but he obviously couldn't hear us because as we all stood and watched, he just slammed into this mound of solid mud at about 50mph. He must have flown 15/20ft in the air before landing on his head and the bike came down onto its back wheel and bounced over him. We called an ambulance and everybody waited with him whilst I got rid of the bike by hiding it in the shed. I ran all the way back to where the accident had happened and the ambulance was there. Dave had long blond hair that came past his shoulders and 'get this,' as the paramedics picked him up, all of his hair stayed on the tarmac. EVERY STRAND! It had all fallen out through shock.! It was the weirdest thing I had ever seen sober He was in the hospital for a while but he was fine, and yes his hair did grow back, just not as long. Me and Billy Wells used to call him 'the scatty chicken' and we used to make him do 'the scatty chicken dance'; fuck me, it was hilarious to watch. He hated doing it but you could see he loved making us laugh. He just didn't like it when we forced him to do it in front of girls, but he had no choice otherwise he would get 'a dig' (a punch). We loved it, he didn't.

Me, Billy and Kev, the fella who very first warned me of Billy when he started at our school, all went out to find a big powerful bike that three of us could get on and believe it or not, we found one. I don't know the model or make I just know it was a 250cc engine and when you're only a kid that's quite powerful. So, we are all on it and Billy (the crazy cunt) is driving (yeah, great) but at that age, you have no fear for some reason. We were approaching a bend in the road and we were travelling at some speed and all I heard from Billy was, "We're not gonna make it, we're not gonna make it!"

I could see and feel that we were not going to make it around this massive bend as we were going too fast. We hit the curb and obviously all three of us came flying off the bike with no crash helmets on or anything. We were lucky to land on some one's front garden (soft grass). Thankfully, nobody was hurt but the lady that lived in the house came out and shouted at Billy, "I know you, your name's Billy Wells!"

He replied, "No it ain't, my name's Dave Trotter," (the scatty chicken) as we were running away, leaving the bike as a gift on her nice front lawn with chunks of turf taken out by the bike.

"Look at it as a new lawn ornament… See ya!!!"
Now things were going to get much darker In my life, so much so that playing on motorbikes would feel like a dream away.

Now… 'PACMAN', wow what a ride that was. And I'm not talking about the 80s computer game either. Was I finally going to gain my 'gangster status'? And if so…at what cost? This geezer's real name was Cassius, well, that's what he told me anyway once I got to know him. Should I have? Well, I'll let you decide. He was a massive black fella dripping in gold, covered in tattoos and looked as fucking hard as they come. This bloke looked so fucking scary that when he looked in a mirror, it screamed. I got given his number by a friend who told me he'd turned up in Basildon today and he was selling 0.4 instead of 0.2 of heroin and crack for a score, (£20) so I'd be getting double for my money. Sweet! I wasn't going to turn that down, was I? What addict would?! So, from Craylands only phone box I called the infamous 'Pacman'. This was the beginning of something huge, I just didn't know it. When he answered, I said, "Pacman, my name's Fisher. I got your number off Greeny can you link me?" (meet me?)

He knew where I was; he must have had the phone box number logged in his phone. He said, "What you after boss?"

I said, "Two white and two brown, please fella."

He replied, "Stay there. I'll be two minutes."

I thought, *Yeah right, if it's anything like normal dealers, I'll be waiting here for half an hour*. Literally two minutes passed and this, as I said before, 'scary looking geezer' came up to me.

"You Fisher?" he said.

I said, "Yeah bruv, two of each, yeah?"

He passed me the gear, two balls of heroin and two of crack. I passed him the eighty pounds, he passed me a score back and told me it was a deal for my first meeting with him. He knew full well that after I had smoked the crack, that 20 quid would go straight on another rock (in his pocket) and he said, "I'm on twenty-four hours a day, bruv, call me."

I said, "I will soon fella," knowing I'd have to score again tomorrow the latest if I didn't get more money on the day. He winked at me, turned and walked away. I was intrigued by him and I think he was by me too. I wasn't the average smack head (heroin addict), I was smartly dressed at all times to begin with, wearing expensive trousers and shirts with flash cufflinks looking sharp and came across like I didn't give a fuck about anyone or anything. I wasn't fazed by this big black fella from London, I wasn't intimidated by him at all. I wanted to be his friend, or should I say associate? I was attracted to money especially 'big and easy' money, and I could sense this fella had dough. So, I thought to myself, *I need to get as much customer to this 'Pacman' as I can and get to know him.*

How could I do this? I started hitting all the hotspots in Basildon for the smackheads. All I had to do was go to all the phone boxes, that's where they tended to congregate together, easy. I'd tell them I could get them a 0.3 for twenty pounds, it's thirty quid's worth, not one of them would turn it down. So, first, I was taking a 0.1 for myself off of every one of them, which is a tenner's worth and second, I was getting to know 'Pacman' and bringing him A LOT of custom and money but this was again, just the start of something much, much bigger. Pacman took a liking to me after just a few weeks. He could see I was well known and accepted by most people in the area. I'd go as far as to say I was quite well-liked and had a lot of friends, just the wrong type of friends (most would say) but I got off on the 'gangster' lifestyle and being feared by others – I fucking loved it! Pacman picked up on this I'm sure, it was his life at the end of the day, it was his job, his living. The first time I knew Pacman sort of liked me was one day when I was sitting in a crowd, again on the infamous Craylands estate There were about twelve of us, I was 'clucking' (going cold turkey). I was bent up in two, doubled up in pieces from the stomach pains of not having what had become my daily medicine, heroin. Pacman was passing and spotted me in the crowd, he called over, "Fisher, you cool, blud?"

I said, "Nah bruv, I'm fucking up over here."

He said, "Come here."

So I hobbled over to him holding my stomach. He said, "What's up with you, cuz?" *As if he didn't know*!

I said, "I'm clucking too hard to go on the earn (on the thieve) and get some money man. I don't know what to do."

he gave me a score (£20) again and a few phone numbers for people that worked for him, he said, "I haven't got anything on me but there's some money to get sorted. Make sure it comes back to me, ya get me? Is that enough?"

I said, "Course bruv, without a doubt, I'll use one of your boys. Thank you so much man."

He said, "I'll see you soon," and off he went. All my mates were saying, "What the fuck? Why is he giving you money? We're all clucking!"

I knew from that moment I was going to get into something deep with this bloke. I started to score my drugs from the numbers Pacman had given me (his workers); there were three of them, they were just runners. One day, I couldn't get a hold of any of the runners, so I called the original number I had which was for Pacman. He answered and he said to me, "Fisher, I've wanted to see you for a chat, come to my house on Craylands, do you know where I am?"

I said, "Yeah, I've seen you coming out of a house on Southwark path, is that it?"

He said, "Yeah."

So I told him I'd be five minutes. I've got to say walking there, my 'not give a fuck' attitude was on hold. I was worried about what I was walking into, as in my time I'd pissed a lot of people off. I knocked at the door, he opened it and without a word he just left the door open and walked off, so I went in and shut the door. He introduced me to his girlfriend, she didn't say a word the whole time I was there, she kept her nut down. I could sense she was petrified of this fella, well, that was my opinion anyway, that's how it seemed. Pacman told me he was a worker for a bigger organization called 'LOVE OR MONEY' run by a group in Hackney but he was the boss in Essex. He went on to tell me a lot about them, how they are stone-cold killers and they were worth millions upon millions. They had fleets of cars and houses all over London and Essex, my ears pricked up and my eyes widened at that moment. But I asked him why he was having me in his home and telling me all this information. He said he wanted me to work for him, he didn't tell me why me. He groomed me into thinking that he really liked me and would for some reason be my 'back up' on the streets, should I need it. He had a massive bag of skunk on the coffee table and he said to me, "Skin up, ya know we're going to have to have a 'sit down' at some point soon but let's just have a little chat and a smoke first."

A 'sit down' amongst criminals meant you were in it, like it or not, because after the 'sit down' you would then know the plan and this made you a liability and a possible 'leak' but I loved a bit of drama and knew how to keep my mouth shut, so when would this 'sit down' be? and would I have the bollox to go ahead with this it? BUT my nerves had already calmed, I must say, and I was now getting excited, *here we go again*. Dealers just seemed to fucking love me! This was not the loving ecstasy club scene any more though, this was something much, much darker and all done on the streets and in people's homes. These were heroin and crack heads I'd be dealing with too, they were not as so 'happy go lucky' as the pill heads were. What 'Pacman' was going to eventually ask of me was going to put me in a whole world of danger but being a heroin addict, you have no fear or no emotions at all really. I was like a living zombie and was told this time and time again by people. Maybe I came across as a machine to Pacman, I don't know, but all of a sudden I was part of 'LOVE OR MONEY'. Love or money literally meant 'your family or your cash or BOTH, we'll take it'. I had done a lot of things in my life already but was I going to get away with this? Would I be pushed to kill?

Pacman wanted to 'shut down and take out every dealer in Basildon town' and all within a week. So, what was my part going to be? This man and the organisation behind him were powerful. I think even before the 'sit down' happened, I knew what I was going to have to do as I was spoken to just a little about it. It was almost the same as the club scam we had, only this was on a much bigger scale and much more dangerous. I had to first find all the dealers and where they lived, how would I do this? Again, I'd hit all the smackheads 'hotspots' and 'hangouts'. I'd get numbers from them for other dealers then Pacman would give me money to go and score off the other dealer's (most of the time the gear was shit and the deals were tiny). So I'd score and then follow them home on the sneaky one to find out where they lived. I did this for a few weeks and I'd gathered fifteen addresses to report back to Pacman, the next step was something I was used to too and used to get a buzz out of too. But times had changed, people lived tooled up with things like gas and guns and big fuck-off machetes. Things were about to get dangerous once again. Pacman called me and demanded I come around. I thought I'd done something wrong from the tone of his voice, he was acting/sounding different. I got ready and went straight to his house, I only lived a ten-minute walk away from him. Today would be the day I would be told all the details of the plan and meet 'the firm, LOVE OR MONEY.

When I arrived and knocked at the door, some fella I'd never seen before opened it and said, "Come in, bruv," (he was an average looking white fella). I shook his hand as I walked in and he said to me, "How you doing, mate? My name's Jim, people call me 'White Boy'."

I said, "Sweet, thanks bruv. Where's Cassius?" meaning, 'Pacman'.

He said, "He's just through there mate with the others." I was for once, shitting myself. I didn't know what to expect; this lot were fucking naughty it turned out. 'White Boy' was Pacman's partner, anyway I went through to the living room there were about five or six blokes there sitting around the dining room table. I felt like this was just like something from a fucking movie, 'a proper sit down'. I felt tense and anxious as Pacman told me to pull out a chair to sit at the table. The first person he introduced me to was a short very stocky black fella named 'Chaos'. I take it it was a nickname, he was also Pacman's boss. He looked like he was in the gym twenty-four hours a day, the fella! This really was another/different criminal underworld at its biggest. I was now in deep for meeting this bloke and seeing his face. I was told under no circumstances did I ever mention his name so I have stuck to my word to this day and I have changed all names including his! But come on, it has been about fourteen years but I will still keep my mouth shut, and let's face it who's going to read this anyway?

'White Boy' sat next to me, 'Chaos' was sat at the head of the table with a pair of what looked like very expensive shades on and dressed from head to toe in an expensive three-piece suit. He was telling me how he had his own private car showroom from vintage cars right up to up to date very expensive 'hypercars'.

"All in black," he said he had three homes with three different women, basically trying to make me think that I could have the same from working for them. I'd been here before just not on this scale. Shit…there was no way out now. All those years of acting like a bad boy were all about to come back and bite me in the arse, as now I had to put my money where my mouth is and be a true 'bad boy'. There were a few others there like I said before, one mixed-race fella called 'matey'. Oh my god, what a fucking plum this geezer was, he thought he was a right gangster because he was involved in this plan, little did he know 'Pacman' thought he was a dick head too. He was the disposable one, but would he keep his mouth shut if he got nicked? I didn't like him and didn't trust him at all. He tried intimidating me but as soon as I felt comfortable, I stood up acting my usual self and I think the roles reversed rapidly and I ended up intimidating him, he stayed seated and kept his mouth shut. I had to let the bosses know I weren't some mug! One of the other fellas that would be pulling off this 'plan' was another white bloke called 'Scottish Dan', now this was a bloke that I already sort of knew through other heroin addicts. I'd been around Dan's house before. After this, we would end up good friends, me and Dan. And I'd find out some shocking things about him later on. He was also an addict to both the heroin and crack, just like me. 'Matey' was on both too but I think every one of us thought he was a plum like I said 'Matey' was a throwaway.

So... The plan was... fifteen dealers in no more than seven days, that was only two a day. I had been prepping myself and thinking long and hard about this plan and therefore suggested we needed to do this quicker, as I knew Basildon well and knew that once we hit a few the others would catch on, hear about it and move their gear fast (heroin and crack plus cash). 'Chaos' and 'Pacman' loved this idea and loved my enthusiasm. I'd been around dangerous people before in my life, I was not fazed or scared or even anxious about this 'plan'. I wanted to do them all in TWO days. To me it made sense, the first day we'd hit half of them so the chances of the others hearing were slimmed down, everybody agreed. *Fuck me, I'd just made a decision for 'LOVE OR MONEY' I hope it works out!*.

I'd told them about the days I used to kick peoples doors in just for fun, so that was it, I was the nominated door kicker. '*Shit, I put myself in it there,* never mind it would be more fun I suppose. At least this time I was getting paid for it with enough heroin and crack to feed my habit and more. Plus, if I needed cash, 'Pacman' would just give it to me. I never wanted to be a dealer for 'Pacman' though I had the option, I chose not to. You may think this is rather contradictory but I never wanted to or agreed with the supply of heroin, it ripped families apart, including mine for a while later on. As if it wasn't already, it would get worse! And here's me helping up set up a heroin/crack empire in Basildon, hypocritical, I know, but the power and reputation that came with what I was about to do felt immense.

So, in three days' time, me and 'Pacman's' crew 'Love or Money' were going to do this. Fifteen dealers, family or not, were about to get a fucking wakeup call of their lives. Only, instead of the police raiding them, unfortunately, it would be 'LOVE OR MONEY'. If we came through your door, you better give up everything you've got or someone's getting fucking shot or cut. That's just how it had to be. 'Pacman' wanted to take over and I was willing to help him. This was not about getting people's drugs off of them, this was about closing down the other dealers to end up the only firm around taking 99% of the customers wherever they went. The night before the day we were doing the first lot, I can't say I slept well, though I was looking forward to proving myself to these hardcore gangsters. I was most definitely shitting myself! 'Pacman' wouldn't tell me any real information about how this was going to happen until the day we were actually doing the job. We were not going to hit the first bloke out of eight that day until early evening.

It was the height of summer, and the evenings (the best time to work), were long. Ideally, you want to do these jobs in the dark but the days were long at the time being summer. 'Pacman' stood out like a sore thumb and looked like trouble from a mile away dripping in gold and tattooed up from head to toe so we favoured the evening under the cover of darkness. I got to 'Pacman's' house the day it was on early evening. Shit, this is really happening. I'm about to go door kicking again, only this time it wasn't unsuspecting people all loved up on pills, these were going to be people that were tooled up themselves to protect themselves from people like us. I don't think a 'rock in a sock' is going to cut it here somehow, though I still had one on me. I asked 'Pacman' what I was going to use for the job when we went through the doors? He passed me a gun… It was a semi-automatic pistol, I didn't

114

know if it was real and if so, was it loaded? I didn't want to insult anyone or embarrass myself by asking. (I now know it was real), these people didn't seem the mickey mouse type, apart from not wanting to look thick, I didn't really care if it was real or not, it looked the part and had a lot of fucking weight to it. I was not planning on pulling the trigger on this job. I was hoping the sight of the gun would be enough for these dealers to do as they were told and if it weren't, I'd fucking hit them in the face with it, simple. Would you argue with six fucking nutters screaming at you in your own home pointing guns when your family and young children are standing there? I know I wouldn't. Yeah, let's fucking do this but fuck the targets; if I get caught by the old bill holding a gun, I'm going down for life, that's 15 years minimum. But... I'm up for it and if I have to pull the trigger then so be it! (At the time of writing this story and for the years leading up to now, I have 'wonky moments' where I switch and don't give a shit about the consequences, this is not the case all of the time though and hopefully by the time this book comes out I'll be better.)

The first flat we arrived at to turn over was a fella I won't name but we gathered around his front door and I listened through the letterbox to try and hear what was what and where people were as the flat was tiny inside. This was one particular dealer that asked me to come to his address to score before, so I knew the layout and knowing this would be the easiest job and he had very few connections to wise up; we, or I, put him first on the list. I could see through that he was on the sofa and his missus was in the kitchen, his two kids were in the living room too with their daddy playing on the floor. 'LOVE OR MONEY' meant exactly that, if he didn't want his loved ones hurt, he would do as instructed with no fuss and fucking give up the lot, I mean I'd done my homework on this firm and they were fucking ruthless and anything went. I kicked the door to the council flat, it went with two kicks in rapid progression. We rushed in there shouting, "LOVE OR MONEY, stay still and tell us where the fucking gear and money is before you get fucking hurt!!"

This would, that day, become a trademark of our attacks or 'raids'. We would shout it on every job so that people knew who they were done by and therefore know not to fuck about with the firm. One of the boys grabbed the missus and dragged her into the living room with a knife to her throat. I rushed to the sofa with the gun in my hand pointing it at point-blank range at the bloke's face and I was screaming, "Fucking stay where you are, don't you fucking move you cunt or I'll fucking shoot ya. Now where are your fucking phones, you MUG?"

I didn't need to ask where his gear and cash was, it was all out on the coffee table for the taking, (and with kids about, shame on him ha-ha, "sorry") actually we were doing him a favour. I screamed at him alongside 'Pacman' telling him he was NEVER to sell crack or heroin in Basildon or Essex ever again and if he did, his Mrs would get it in front of him and then it'd be him after as he watched! His kids would be left with no parents! This was harsh but bloody effective as you can imagine. He swore he would never sell again in the area and all his customers would be sent to 'Pacman's' runners. We took his drugs, his money and left him with a few numbers and the shakes. We were only in there about five minutes if that.

The rest of the evening was much the same, we hit another seven people and we didn't have one problem, nobody was prepared for us and not one dealer refused to give up their drugs and cash or even try to fight back, they were all petrified. The only problems we faced, were that some of the doors were tougher to get through taking that extra few seconds which can be vital in a raid. But with a crowbar and a couple of 18-stone geezers, not one of the doors could keep us out. We had one scary-looking fucking bunch of blokes, I mean I get told that I am scary-looking, but these geezers were twice the size of me and looked so fucking mean even scrooge would have handed his money belt over. We had closed down half of Basildon's dealers in one day (more than the bloody old bill could ever do). 'Pacman' must have taken at least 80 thousand pounds I guess, if not more. He let us smackheads working for him, share out the gear we had accumulated throughout the raids, there was only three of us working that were actually on it so we had loads and I was very conservative with my heroin as it becomes your medicine and you need it every day just to function and be 'normalish'.

I was known not to abuse my heroin and to use it like medicine, as I didn't know that I was taking heroin when I got hooked as you know. I was known for 'being tight' with it but for one, I didn't like giving it to people, it's wrong, *(I know right?! After what I've just done)* and two, I was just using it wisely as medicine and nothing more. So I didn't let it get wildly out of control, the crack was a different story though. I could do a thousand pounds in a matter of hours, literally. I fucking absolutely loved it!

The next day we were to do the same again only this time it was someone else's turn to hold the gun, thank fuck. The drill was the same but the risks today were higher as obviously, other dealers had heard. So, run in make sure you know where everyone in the house is and get them gathered in one room then just scream and shout a lot, look fucking crazy and just really scare these people into handing everything over – drugs, cash and even phones so that their lines were turned off. We were closing down dealer's ready to set up an empire that would end up making millions each day and hundreds of millions over a short period of time, but how would it all end because let's face it, everything comes to an end at some point, and would I end up with anything apart from a bigger 'habit' or a prison sentence?

All the time we were planning these raids, 'Pacman' had been recruiting 'runners', people to sell his supply of heroin and crack for him who drove so they could be a delivery service. With only one firm running Basildon for its crack and smack surely now there would be less of it about, right? You would think so but no… Basildon was about to be absolutely flooded with the shit. *Oh FUCK, what have I done?* And because the deals were 0.4 for twenty quid instead of 0.2, peoples habits were doubling and spiralling out of control, including mine. Pacman's 'firm' was now the only business running in Basildon and it was all down to me. The 'plan' had worked, I was now a well-respected member of 'LOVE OR MONEY'. I had set them up to take over! I felt like a fucking king until 'Pacman' made it clear we were not the best of mates or anything, but if I needed him for anything he would be there to help me. I now had back up on the streets to the point where one day I called one of the boss' runners named 'Matey' (remember him? The plum, the disposable one). He gave me a load of verbal over the phone and told me to come to his house. When I got there he hung out of his kitchen window with a crack pipe in his hand and blew the fucking smoke in my face and told me to fuck off (he was too busy on the crack and all fucked up on it). So I called the boss (Pacman) he said, "I'm at the lakes with my missus and my kid meet me there now and I'll call him and sort it."

I went and see 'Pacman' and I was ill and needed some heroin badly! 'Pacman' made a call he simply said, "Matey, lakes, two minutes." The lakes were at the back of Matey's house. Matey came running literally out of breath and asking, "What's the emergency?"

Pacman grabbed Matey up by the collar lifting him clean off of the floor and went fucking crazy at him saying, "Look, you little cunt, these boys pay for everything I own and even the clothes that my baby is wearing! You fucking look after this boy or I'll fucking cut ya face off and put you in that fucking lake! Now sort him out right now and never fuck him about again, RIGHT?"

Matey apologised and went all sheepish. I never had a problem dealing with him again and he even invited me into his home for a pipe in the kitchen whilst his kids were in the next room. Pacman's firm ended up consisting of loads of people who were all selling massive amounts of heroin and crack, obviously, and they were handing over the profits to Pacman at the end of every single day. So, let me give you some idea of what they were earning for him – the 'smaller dealers' were taking around about two grand (£2000) profit a day to hand over so four grand (£4000) including what had to be put back in a day. The others, who were working twenty-four hours a day with their phones always on at any time, were probably taking about eight to ten thousand pounds a day,

EACH! There were loads of them all together that adds up to roughly £70.000 a day PROFIT and £140,000 altogether, every day at the very minimum and that was just the start as it only took a few weeks to get to this stage (that's nearly one million pound a week). That's fucking ridiculous amounts of money Pacman was taking; he was fucking having it off mate. He bought himself a big flash motor all in black, I think it was a BMW. He had a baby with a woman that lived on Craylands (the estate I'd ruled with my mates for years), even the police stayed away from this estate. 'LOVE OR MONEY' were getting too big and too flash, I just knew they couldn't carry this on forever, it had to come to an end at some point.

So, to be honest, I started to distance myself from the firm altogether. I was robbing other dealers so I didn't need to contact them and if I wanted the bigger deals from that lot, I would get one of my pals to go to them for me to save any more interaction with the firm, they were getting too fucking hot. Eventually, after a bloody good run, a good year or two must have passed and the inevitable happened. 'LOVE OR MONEY' were simultaneously raided and arrested all in one morning. I'd got out just in time. People were even saying, "I was a grass!" Fucking hell, I just could see what was going to happen and I used my head and was not greedy. It was a good old school friend of mine nicknamed 'Ropey' who fucked everything up and put the final nail in the coffin for 'LOVE OR MONEY' by selling to a police officer (C.I.D). But apparently, this copper tried a bit of the gear to prove to the firm he wasn't old bill… It had been said that he had been smoking daily for a few weeks with 'Ropey' and I heard he took a bit of a liking for it and ended up thrown off the force and placed in rehab to beat his newfound addiction. It can grab fucking anyone. Anybody can get hooked, but this was to be the end of the Essex branch of 'LOVE OR MONEY' they had been shut down in one morning by the bigger firm, the police. Let's face it, they are practically unbeatable. They are really the only people I've ever been consistently afraid of as the courts can just take your life away in the blink of an eye. I'd escaped prison all my life and certainly wasn't even thinking of going now. 'Ropey' was probably the lowest key dealer for 'Pacman', I think he got about three to four years and at the other end of the scale, 'Pacman' himself, when they found out which one was 'Pacman', received about fourteen years I think, maybe more but did they have the right man?

Back, just before these arrests though, obviously other random dealers would still spring up in Basildon weekly whilst 'Pacman's' firm was working, so knowing I had the 'back up', I used to just rob them on the street of my own accord as a little extra bunce for myself. This is how I started to carry on feeding my habit for a while as I thought this was the best thing to do. It was not like they could go the police now, is it? And they weren't innocent victims, they were scumbags who were dealing this shit to kids. I became known to rob new dealers and when people turned up to deal in Basildon they were often warned about me by the other smackheads.

"Don't deal to Fisher, he'll rob you," they'd be told and often they would turn up mob-handed to meet me. One morning me and a pal I had working with me as a driver to get us to work tiling. We were both feeling ill one day as neither of us had saved any heroin from the night before, so what could we do. Well…my pal, on the way to work at seven in the morning, decided to pop into his family-run business. I didn't know why or what he was doing. About ten minutes passed, as I waited in the car, all of a sudden, he came running out of the building with a red cloth money bag. He jumped in the driver's side and threw me the bag as he slammed the car into reverse and pulled away fucking sharpish. He said to me, "Look in there, I don't think it's anything though."

I felt the bag it, felt like empty money bags like thin plastic bags but then I opened it. It was full of cash! The bag was half full. Work all of a sudden went to the bottom of our list of priorities. We had to score some crack and smack asap. The only blokes I knew that would be on at that time in the morning called themselves Jesus and Moses. They knew I was a 'dealer robber' and despite the relationship I had with their boss (Pacman), they still didn't trust me, especially as I was calling them at quarter past seven in the morning asking for 10 white and 10 brown and telling them I was willing to pay full price if they would meet me quick, as I had work, but 10 white and 10 brown amounts to £400. These boys were thinking all sorts, ha, who would blame them? They said to me that they had the gear but they couldn't meet me for 45 minutes. I was asking why? They wouldn't give me an answer they just said they had to wait for someone. I knew what was going on, they were thinking I was out to rob them.

Anyway, 45 minutes passed and they turned up mob-handed with five big fucking black fellas almost as if to say, 'Yeah, try it'. I just laughed and handed over the £400 cash and took the gear. I said, "Oi, oi, there's fucking loads of ya, what did you think I was gonna rob ya or something? Hahaha."

They just said, "Bruv, can you blame us?" *(I suppose not).*

Me and my pal drove straight to the job and pulled up outside. We got all the tools off the car and set up to tile a disabled toilet in a brand-new office block on the Festival Leisure Park in Basildon.

Problem...

As soon as I had set up, before starting, I had a crack pipe in the car, now anyone that knows about it will know that as soon as you do one, you need another within about thirty seconds if not less, which meant the chances of me starting work anytime soon was, well...slim to say the very least. At least until the rock was all gone. So that's what happened, me and my mate sat in his car and smoked £200 worth of crack in about the space of an hour. The problem now was that I was too prang (which is the feeling you get when you run out). It's a feeling you can't explain apart from the fact you just need more and more and you cannot think or function on anything else but that, unless you take heroin to bring you back down. It's a vicious circle if EVER I've been in one. So now I was in no fit state to work, so I packed all my tools away back into the car and pulled a 'sickie'. Went back to my pal's and got smacked up. Sad. It was a few days later, and me and this pal had the same problem as the other day. We were skint and clucking (cold turkey for heroin), so I had a scummy plan in mind. We would go to the site I was supposed to be working on that day in Rayleigh Essex but we would be late. 10:30am, break time for builders. We waited for them to all go to the canteen and we quickly grabbed all the most expensive tools there, which were all the woodwork tools mainly like saws and heavy-duty drills. We loaded up the boot of the car and fucked off. I had buyers for anything and everything and at any time of day. So we went straight round my tool man's

123

house to sell them. There must have been at least a grand's worth of tools if not more. It was all 'DeWalt' and 'Makita' and 'Bosch', all the big names at the time. We got £200, £100 each – when you're a heroin addict that's plenty for the day. We went straight to score and then parted ways for the day. Later on, I get a call from my boss and he tells me, doing what we had done, he had to sack me. That was the end of that bit of legal work and on top of this, the fella who was working for me and stole the tools with me and also took half of the money, wanted payment from me still. As you can imagine I told him there was no fucking chance, we did the crime together so we both pay for it. Now back to a life of crime again I suppose until someone else takes me on. If they ever do.

I was deep into heroin now and I was truly addicted. I had been for fucking ages now but what people don't understand is, as I understand it, your brain releases/creates a certain chemical that is sent to all your muscles in your body to stop cramp and anxiety and restless leg syndrome amongst other things. The opiates in heroin replace this chemical and therefore your brain realises the chemical is being put into your body manually and so it stops producing it. So, if you do heroin for seven days in a row, your brain will stop producing the chemical needed. Then when you don't have the heroin/chemical to put in, your body is missing the natural muscle relaxant you need. Your whole body starts to 'cramp up', it really is pure agony coupled with vomiting and not being able to control your bowels properly. This EVIL stuff becomes your medicine. Literally! It's not so much a mental addiction. It is a physical addiction more so. You need it just to stop your cramps and pains from kicking in and forcing you into a crumpled mess on the floor being sick and shitting yourself at the same time, and I do mean literally. How the fuck would I ever get off this stuff? I obviously knew by now I had hit an all-time low being on heroin, so I tried my best to keep it from Carisa and I had hidden it well from most people but you can't hide being on that stuff forever, especially when you get right into it and get 'out ya nut'. You cannot hide the piercing evil eyes and the major slurred speech. Not to mention the constant scratching yourself as it makes you really itchy too. What looked appealing about this, I don't know but Carisa wanted a go of it despite my protests. So yeah...I fucked up... I gave it to her.

Being in a co-dependent relationship too makes it twice as hard to get clean. What had I done? Now it was my duty to protect this girl. Yeah, hypocritical, right? People spread vicious rumours that I had got her on it to keep her and control her which I can swear to this day, on all that I own, that was not true. If anything, once Carisa found out I was on the smack and how it would affect my life and keep me hidden from the world, she was all up for it. So much so that one of the many, many times I attempted to get clean from the drug whilst living with my mum, Carisa was caught by my mum and stepdad bringing heroin into the house to give to me all the while they were thinking I'm going cold turkey in my bedroom. I was putting it on and taking the smack that was being smuggled in by the one that was supposed to care for me.

When my mum caught her after clocking my eyes weren't right and searching her, she asked Carisa why was she bringing it in? My mum went on to say that Carisa must have wanted to keep me on it for whatever reason, she understood but why? So my mum put it cleverly to Carisa, eventually getting the answer from Carisa who said, "Yes, Wendy, I like him being on it because for one, other girls are not looking at him and two, he spends all of his time just with me lately."

I was violent with Carisa from the start and regularly got physical with her as I did all the girls I got with and mates, which would continue a long time into the future but would it ever stop? Would I ever stop? And WHY was I like that? Well, remember the first real bout of violence towards a female was with Jaida when I thought she had a black man down the side of the bed and then trying to get out of the window? Well, that was obviously all down to the drugs even though I was stone-cold sober at that precise moment. It was ultimately down to the class As I had been abusing massively. Ever since then I had a sort of voice in my head, sometimes more than one at a time too. A question I often get asked is, "Was it your own voice talking to you?" and the answer is 'No'. It was an overpowering male voice inside of my head that obviously only I could hear. He used to tell me that people were lying to me, and 'mugging me off' was his favourite phrase.

"They are mugging you off, Fisher! They are lying to you too!"

Then what started happening (and what would shape my future for many years to come) was, I would ask somebody a question, for whatever reason and I would already have the answer I thought that they should reply with in my head. So, if they didn't reply with the exact words I had in my head previous to the question being asked by me, then the voice would kick in and tell me that I was being lied to. In turn, I would then feel belittled and I would lose my temper and it

126

could be with absolutely anybody – mother, friend, girlfriend, shopkeepers, bus drivers, literally anyone. Would this voice ever stop? or would it get worse and worse and control my life forever?

One of the most undesirable characters I remember that I would meet along the 'brown mile' (heroin path) I had taken, would be when I was working in Bromley by Bow in London. One morning I had overdone it with my smack the night before and not saved any, so I woke up ill and after travelling for an hour on the train with all my tools, I was fucking clucking hard. I had noticed the day before a few Indian boys in the stairwells of the flats we were refurbishing, smoking smack, so I was just going to ask them, but I got to the job and set my tools up and the boys were nowhere to be seen. As the morning progressed, after about an hour I got more and more ill and had gotten no work done as I was in and out of the flat I was supposed to be working in to try and bump into the boys so I could ask them to score for me. I had no joy so I decided to go for a walk and see if I could spot anyone who looked like they might take heroin as they are not hard to spot. After about an hour of hanging around a local phone box close to the site where I was supposed to be working, along came a fella who was unmistakably a smackhead into the phone box and pulled out a list of numbers on a piece of paper. This was also another sure sign, so I said to him, "Oi mate, can you get any brown?"

He replied, "I can get you brown, white, pink, blue or green. I can get you all the colours of the rainbow if you got the money, boy."

He was an older fella I suppose, in his late 50s maybe, even 60s. He was a tiny little bloke as skinny as you could imagine. He was balding on top with long black real thin hair and a big bushy black beard. He looked well rough. I was fucking over the moon. I had found a way of getting some gear so I could carry on at work the day instead of packing up and going home. Or at least after I had had a smoke. He asked me how much I wanted so I told him I had twenty quid on me, so he ordered me a twenty ball which now days was a .4 of a gram in London. Enough to last me 24 hours easily and get me through work for the day. I stepped in the phone box to hear the conversation on the phone to ensure I wasn't getting ripped off. I heard him order it and the geezer on the other end of the phone saying he would be ten minutes. So I asked this bloke his name and where he lived? He told me his name was Clyde and coincidently, he lived on the estate we were working on so his flat would be one I would be tiling once getting around to it. So, Clyde invited me to his flat, number 80, and we went in to wait for the heroin and crack that he had ordered for me and for himself. He introduced me to his wife who also looked really ill and worn out and was obviously also a heroin addict. Either that or her paper round was all uphill, shhh, shouldn't laugh.

Ten minutes passed and a little Pakistani fella turned up with our gear to the front door. Brilliant I didn't run the risk of even being seen scoring. I asked if I could stay for 20 minutes or so and smoke a bit of gear so that I could get back to work before someone noticed that I had done 'fuck all' so far that day. Clyde said. "Yeah, no problem."

So that's what I did. I did just enough heroin to stop my aches and pains but not too much so as I couldn't work. Then I went back to work in another part of the estate. I returned a few more times to Clyde's place first thing in the mornings and had a coffee and a smoke with him before starting work that day, but I never saw him taking his own heroin. I saw him smoke crack and he told me that he injected his heroin but he didn't let me see him and later on with time I would find out why. I finished early one Friday afternoon and I went to Clyde's as my bosses had been to the site and dropped our wages off to us in cash. I bought him some gear as a treat for helping me recently. We smoked the crack and it only lasted about an hour and I moved straight onto my brown (heroin). Clyde seemed reluctant to do his even though he knew that I knew he used needles for it. I didn't get it until I saw what I saw next. Clyde could hold out no longer he asked his wife 'to do it'. After cooking up his heroin on the spoon and drawing it into his syringe she wrapped her hands around the bottom of his neck as he stretched it out and then proceeded to stick the needle in the top of his neck/throat. He said this was necessary because every other vein in his body had collapsed due to 40 years of injecting heroin, crack and pretty much anything he could get his hands on, melt down and put into a needle to inject directly into his veins. He was putting the needle in and out, in and out and still could not get a vein. So, his missus grabbed him even tighter around the throat/neck until a vein in his forehead popped up and then I watched this little geezer inject directly into his fucking head. This was one of the craziest things I had ever seen, and I had seen a lot. Monday morning, I was called into the site manager's office as he apparently wanted a word. I just assumed it was snagging on my work or something, nothing to worry about right? Wrong! I had been seen coming and going from number 80 and I said, "Yeah, what's the problem? The fella's a friend, I know him!"

The site agent went on to tell me that number 80 had been refused work done to it by all contractor's because when somebody went up on the outside to measure the windows they had seen exactly what I had seen with my own eyes the Friday before. Clyde jacking up in his HEAD. So anyway, because they had seen me with Clyde and seen me coming and going to and from his flat, they, therefore, quite rightly came to the conclusion that I was using heroin at work. So I was sacked and asked to get my tools and leave the site immediately and my bosses would be informed. Great another job gone. Not that I really cared for that job as when I was pulling out refrigerators and ovens etc. The places were running alive with cockroaches and bugs, it was fucking horrible. So I told my bosses that that was why I was leaving this site in the shear hope the site agent would just leave it and keep it to himself as I had agreed with him not to come back, but no such luck, unfortunately, the inevitable happened and they told my bosses. Another well-paid job down the lavvy.

To be honest, what with all the travelling around London every day on trains and buses just to get to a job with all my tools, I fucking hated it. I knew of easier money and I wanted it again!

One night there was a crowd of about eight of us just loitering around Basildon on the streets looking for a motorbike to nick and sell. We all had tiny amounts of heroin on us but we knew it wouldn't be long and we would need more, plus a crack pipe right now wouldn't go amiss! So we were looking for 'an earner'. We walk past the back of the fishing tackle shop, I won't say which one. One of my pals who was big into burglary noticed a small-sized metal grate, like a vent leading into the back of the building. He said, "If we can get that off I can squeeze in there!"

We said, "Fuck off, bruv, it's tiny" and he wasn't a small lad! Anyway, he pulled out a flathead screwdriver (that he took everywhere with him) and proceeded to try and prize this metal from the wall. Eventually, after us all going to work on it and in about 45 minutes, we were in. Well, 'Jez' was. He had got straight into the stockroom and fishing gear is worth fucking loads of money to a bunch of smackheads like us. Jez shouted through, "Go and get me a Phillip's screwdriver, this one's no good."

We didn't ask what for, just two of us ran to the closest of our houses which was Luke Nevendon's, got one and ran all the way back making Jez wait in the back of the shop risking tripping a silent alarm for 20 minutes but that's how long it took us to get back with it. He then unscrewed the contact/magnetic alarms on the rear door so that they didn't separate and laid them on the floor still touching so that the alarm did not go off. We opened the doors wide, it was about midnight so nobody was around that area at that time of night because of us anyway, so the chances of being seen by anyone who might be considered a witness was slim. So, like I said, we had the doors open and now we needed somewhere to stash all the gear. So the eight of us got everything we possibly could out and stashed it somewhere until we could go back and put it on the market for sale without arousing suspicion that it was us obviously. But where we stashed it couldn't have been funnier. The next morning the place was flooded with the old bill, the owner was doing his nut and we had all caught wind of it and come to watch what was going on. Just like they say, 'they always return to the scene of the crime.' We watched them search high and low for some of sort of clue which may help them find out where the stuff had gone, as in what direction even but…nothing. The best part of it to me was behind the fishing shop were a load of old half-broken-down garages, with walls down and doors missing and that sort of thing. Well, one of the garages (the third one away from the shop) was in reasonable condition so we put all the stuff in there and screwed the doors back on, it was magic, or should I say hilarious to us. It was right under their noses the whole time. We left it for 24 hours, waited for it to get dark and two at a time went and cleared out the garage that was no more than 25 metres away from the shop! Huh. We did well out of that. I think we ended up with about £350 each for fuck all. That's a nice size crack session and heroin for after. Heaven, yeah? Nah…HELL! Try and get away from it. You will only be pulled further in, please trust me.

Things got so bad at home that my mum had no choice but to throw me out onto the streets armed with a letter for the council to say she could no longer have me under her roof. Things were easier back then though as I remember it still took quite a while to be housed. I was living rough for about six months, sleeping in the stairwells on the Craylands estate and staying wherever I had an offer for the night (obviously fellow junkies places). I stayed with some extremely dangerous and unhinged people, the smack being the only thing getting me to an unconscious state to be able to sleep and I suppose also gave people a false relationship/friendship if even only for a short while.

One night, in particular, I was sleeping in a stairwell and it was snowing. I was on a concrete floor in just my clothing with no blankets or sleeping bag or even cardboard, nothing!

I got so cold at one point in the night, I needed a piss and disgustingly I pissed myself on purpose just to feel the warmth on my legs for a short moment. The warmth quickly passed and I just felt wet and even more cold and now also stunk of piss with no change of clothes, great. This was an all-time low (at least so far). I felt like the scum of the earth. While I was homeless I stayed with a few different characters. One was Scottish Dan, you've heard me mention him before but as I'm sure you can appreciate, I can't quite remember when exactly I met him and how. Dan's place was a fucking crack den. Him and his missus had about six kids and three dogs, a few cats and birds flying around the house and all sorts – this place was like a fucking jungle. You had to step over the dog shit, and everywhere you walked was a fucking minefield, it was horrendous and it stunk of shit. If I had the option to sleep there I would though, (out of the cold) Dan was on heroin and crack too and anything else he could get his hands on. There was a point I stayed with Dan for about a month, I think. While I was staying there Dan would go out every night, late, and come back three hours later with a massive wedge of cash. I didn't mention anything about it for a couple of weeks. I just sat back each day and waited for the night time to roll around so Dan would go and get the dough to score. It was a sure thing each evening but then eventually, curiosity got the better of me. I had to ask how he was getting these big bundles of cash every night to support his habit and his family, because let's face it when you are a heroin addict, the heroin comes before all. He told me 'quite to my surprise' openly he was a hitman. He went on to tell me how easy it was to kill someone in their sleep quietly. He clearly had no conscience and then he would just simply go and collect a massive wad of cash once 'the job' was done. He seemed stone-cold and completely heartless talking about it as I suppose you would have to be. There was no mention of these people's backgrounds or family or even what they had done wrong, he simply didn't care. It was just 'a job' to Dan and that was it, just a name or a number. He even offered me work saying to me that I would not have to necessarily kill someone, I could take a job beating someone up for a smaller sum of money. But the 'work', as he called it, was always there for me. Dan for some reason respected me and we got along, as he had seen me in action running with 'Pacman's' crew (Love or Money) and knew exactly what I was capable of, and on heroin, I had NO conscience either.

He also ran security at big football events like Wembley for example, concerts etc... He also offered me work there too. I never took any of this dark work on, I would rather take a dealer for everything they have instead, it's a victimless crime and as I see it, I was saving lives even though I was wrecking my own and my family's all at the same time. I also spent a short while with a bloke that I knew as a 'here and there' part time heroin dealer. He just used to dabble in dealing but was a hardcore user and into injecting straight into his veins. Fuck that! His criminal name was Andy, I won't disclose his real name as he is still an active criminal as far as I know and still an addict (if he's still alive). This fella was known to be one nasty piece of work and would cut you to ribbons given half the chance, and I mean just for fun or even just looking at him in the wrong way. Well, certainly, if you had a tenner on you. We bumped into each other whilst scoring our gear off the same bloke and I just mentioned to Andy that I had been sleeping rough, and the same old shit was coming out of my mouth about how I wanted to stop the heroin but I had no help etc. Andy asked me how serious I was about getting off it? He offered for me to go and stay at his for two weeks and he would get me off it. On one condition, I didn't ask him for it once though he would be doing it in front of me. This rule was NOT to be broken according to him. This would be a major task but Andy had promised that he would help me in some way get through it. I was confused as to how he thought he could do this. What did he have some magic fucking beans? Well, yeah in a way (Magic rocks at least). None the less, it was somewhere to stay and I was intrigued by how he was going to help me through! Anyway, we went back to Andy's maisonette on Craylands estate (familiar surroundings to me). Andy said I could leave at any time and pull out but I was NEVER to ask him for help again regarding heroin if I did pull out. We got the 'brown' out we had just bought and we sat on the edge of our seats and smoked the lot. I was on another planet. I was not used to just buying my heroin and doing it all in one go. I used to space it out and literally use it as my medicine to get through each and every day pain-free! The evening rolled around in the blink of an eye. We had been gauging (in and out of consciousness) for hours in silence just listening to the TV. Now the effects were wearing off slightly. I wasn't in pain but heroin 'as always' was on my mind. I didn't ask for it, I dare not, but I did ask what the plan was to keep me going through the cold turkey which lasts seven days more or less? Andy said, "Just give it an hour," this was at midnight.

So as one o'clock rolled around after a few joints of some lovely skunk, Andy said, "Right, get your coat. We're going for a walk, come on."

So I did. We walked for about ten minutes over to an estate I was unfamiliar with and I felt right on edge and fucking full of anxiety. Yeah this geezer I'm with is a nutter but what if someone nuttier than him spots us. Or should I say ME, if I was off my own patch. I was nervous these days as I had done some naughty things and a lot of people would have liked to see me in the ground for sure. He took me to a block I recognised and when we were on the way there he used a name I recognised while he was on the phone. We were going to a crack dealer's. Not only did this geezer sell crack, he manufactured it himself in MASSIVE amounts each time in saucepans and jars making ounces and kilos at a time. I didn't let on that I knew anything, I just kept my mouth shut. I was growing more and more curious as to what Andy's plan was for me. As we approached the block, Andy told me to wait around the corner for him. So, there I am, at just gone one o'clock in the morning, looking as dodgy as fuck outside some very well-known crack dealer's place. Man, I was feeling out of place like a fish out of water and just wanted to get back to the estate I knew and loved, where I felt safe. I had a mate on every block but if they lived with their parents you could bet I wasn't allowed in their home. I waited for about fifteen minutes and Andy appeared from around the corner. He didn't say a word to me, he just walked past me. So I followed him and we went back to his flat. He said he had something to help me. We got back to his and he pulled out enough crack cocaine to last 24 hours. Now that was a big fucking lump; there must have been half an ounce (£800) worth and to a heroin addict that is some amount to have as your personal smoke for the night. We started piping straight away after making a couple of makeshift pipes out of beer cans and using fag ash to rest it on as you burn it – it's actually quite scientific, huh. We smoked crack the entire night and all the next day with the curtains drawn and the TV on in the background while we chatted shit to each other and revealed our life stories to each other whilst buzzing out of our faces. We must have run out at about eight that evening and the feeling of running out after a session like that is so fucking depressing that you literally want to kill yourself and unless you've done it, you could NOT understand. BUT…I wasn't thinking of heroin. Then an hour or so passed and the cold turkey for heroin was starting to kick in but I knew I was at risk of Andy kicking off or kicking me out if I mentioned it. He just kept saying, "Just wait, just wait." Like clockwork, 1 o'clock that night, or early hours in the morning, we went back to the same place and I waited just as same as the night before and the pattern repeated. I had no idea how Andy was getting these massive rocks as he had no money and didn't seem to be selling any of it to cover the cost. This went on for a week and although I was now mentally addicted to crack, I was no longer addicted physically to heroin, at least I don't think I was, but then again I would never know as the first thing I did when I left Andy was go and swap a lump of crack I had lifted from him, for a ball of smack and got straight back on it like a fucking idiot. Thanks for trying Andy, I'll never forget it and I'll see you again if ever I think I can help you.

This was just one of many, many, times I would get clean from smack and go back to it. They don't call it 'Lady H' for no reason. You split from her but you can't live without her! Will I ever fucking get there?

Another 'little earner' was alcohol, but not the sort of alcohol off of the shelves that you can actually get to without hurting anybody. Oh no, it couldn't be that easy, it had to be the spirits which were kept always behind the counter before the days of glass cabinets, but not before the days of alarm tags, unfortunately, so how would we get them? Well, it was simple. 'T' would pull up outside in the Merc (which his mum and dad bought him ironically for 'getting clean') and we would run in, four of us (me, Mark (Richie), Tone and his brother), and grab a basket each and shove the workers who were behind the counter to the floor whilst threatening them if need be as nothing was standing in our way of getting some more smack and crack. We all had Halloween mask's on and would fill up the baskets with expensive booze like whisky, vodka and mainly brandy and off we would run, often chased by the people we had just thrown on the floor, limping. I never got nicked for one of these raids we pulled off and in our time we must have pulled off 50 of them in a couple of months or maybe a few months, it was in the summer I remember that. We had a few 'have a go hero' jobsworth types trying to defend something that didn't even belong to them and what these silly fuckers didn't realise was that the people I was doing this with WOULD HAVE KILLED if pushed too far by stabbing one of these silly idiots trying to protect the company's stock. These people really were putting their lives on the line for their jobs. 'T' only had an old 190E Mercedes on an A plate, but he kept his rims clean, huh (if you know, you know). This car didn't hang about though so by the time they had stopped trying to stop us, and actually called the police, we were long gone and in another town. There weren't automatic number plate readers at the entrance to each town then, thank fuck. Crime was a lot easier back then.

We would drift around a random town out of the area we had just robbed, and wait until we thought it safe to enter into the zones we had to go to sell the drink to get the cash to get the heroin/medicine. I mean can you even imagine what that is like having to live like that every single day? Being somebody who used to be afraid of jail too and even afraid of the police. We knew the hotspots for us (where they would be looking 'the old bill'), and roughly how long it would take to calm down. It generally went on how bad the little job went. Like if somebody got punched or hurt from the shop we would have to go to ground out of the manor for a day or two, but if it was just a simple grab and run whilst laughing and no attempt on anyone stopping us, it would be calm in an hour or two. The old bill were too predictable. They would look in the same places and in the same order every time. I mean, we even used to take the piss and follow a squad car about three cars back, that we knew was looking for us but it was a laugh, silly cunts never ever clocked us. We used to nearly piss ourselves with laughter. We would sit and watch them go to 'T's mum's address where the car was registered and we would just simply follow them until they flew off on another job. Mugs!

We weren't out to hurt anyone. We were ill! Very, very ill! Well, mentally unstable too!

Long before I was homeless and got my bedsit at Ryedene, I worked for a fella who called himself 'white Dave' from Dagenham. I gained this bloke's trust very quickly even for me, by hanging around with him and his little crew of dickheads in the casino in Westcliff daily. I mean this fella used to think nothing of coming out of there £4000 light but then I suppose that's only a day's wage for a smack and crack dealer. He only had to wait for one day to get his money back

– 'easy come, easy go'. I think I was working for him 'shotting' (selling drugs) for about four or five days and I said to him, "Look, Dave, you might as well just hand me the basher phone (work line) and all the gear (smack and crack)." About £2000's worth all together, and guess what? He only agreed. He didn't even know where I lived or hung about or anything. Huh, what a plum. So, yep, you've guessed it. I went missing for two days and smoked the whole lot. He was leaving me voicemails saying he was going to 'carve me up'. Yeah, like I cared.

"Fuck off, you mug."

I even called him and said, "Here Dave, can you tick me a tenner's? I have run right out." and I roared out laughing and hung up to him screaming down the phone at me that he was going to kill me. I didn't think I would ever see him again and then I started to hear stories of how naughty he was, oops. So how do you think I felt when about, however many years later, I live in my own place and as I go to come out my front door on a random day in the summer, his conspicuous purple ford probe car was out the front. I quickly went back in and thought, *Shit, he's found me. He didn't give up. What do I do? I thought, Fuck it, I'll face it.*

So I grabbed myself a Stanley knife and I went out there and down the stairwell towards him. His reaction was shocking. I thought I was walking into a knife fight and it turns out that the fella is moving in two doors away. I approached him and he asked how I was and shook my hand. Then told me if I wanted any 'work' to give him a knock. Yeah, I think I'll swerve going into his place alone, huh. That was it. No drama! No trouble!

When I passed my driving test at the age of 17, I was over the moon. To add to the brilliant achievement, a nice surprise was on its way. I went round to my nan and granddad's house, (my granddad, 'the dream maker') and my grandad said to me, "Well done, boy! Look, me and your nan have decided to give you nan's car."

It was an escort 1.6 gear, it had all the extras and my grandad had bought a big flash spoiler to fit on the back in a couple of weeks and this car was immaculate inside and out, it was like brand new and had only done 28,000 miles. My nan had only ever used it to go to work in and she worked in her home town of Wickford. My grandad threw me the keys and his words were, "This car has not had a dent in it in 11 years, make sure it stays that way."

I was so bloody excited to get in the car and pick my mates up and get to the circuit in Southend. My family told me not to go out of Basildon until I was familiar with the roads etc, blah blah blah, and did I listen? No! I went straight to pick two of my pals up and their girlfriends. So one sat in the front with me and the two girls and the other mate sat in the back. Off we went to the strip on Southend seafront to show off my new car (that wasn't even modified in any way or flash or anything), but I was over the moon with it. It was a fast car for someone that had just passed their test. We went around the circuit a few times then we decided to try and score some weed there or at least some puff (solid cannabis). So my two mates got out of the car to start asking around and I went up some random road and got a little lost with the two girls in the back of the car. We pulled around the back of somewhere I sort of recognised. It was only the palace hotel where I used to work selling drugs. Anyway, I swear I am not racist in the slightest (as I think is clear from the story) but there were a group of black fellas and girls walking casually in the road, so wrongly I hung out the window, put my foot down and shouted, "Get out the fucking road, ya black cunts."

They moved sharpish and disappeared into the multi-story car park. So I spun the car around and I am sitting at red traffic lights and a white BMW screeches up behind me. It was the black fellas and their girls. They were tooting and shouting all sorts of racist abuse at me. (I know I deserved it!) One of the girls in the back of my motor said, "Turn this tune up, I love it."

So I am sat at the light with a group of angry black fellas wanting to beat me, the music is pumping and I suppose I didn't realise my foot was down on the accelerator as I couldn't hear the rev's and as the light turned green, I took my foot off the clutch and the car just fucking flew. I panicked, and instead of stamping on the brake, I stamped on the accelerator and ploughed straight into a wall that surrounded somebody's garden around the front of their house. I got caught between a lamppost and the wall taking down 9 metres in length of the wall too that was built two bricks thick because of it being a hotspot for this happening. Thankfully, instinct took over as the crash happened because I knew the girls were in the back and I locked my arm behind the passenger headrest creating a barrier, into which one of the girls slammed into and hit my arm, hard. So, if my arm hadn't of been there she would have gone through the windscreen and maybe died. I had saved her from possible death or certain injury. My repayment was, her family tried to sue me for her having nightmares of the crash. Come on behave yourself, people. They didn't get far with that as they were warned that though I was young, I was dangerous and not to be fucked with or pissed off, so they stopped pursuing it all of a sudden, after someone posted a few ░onymous notes through the letterbox of their front door o░ ░urse.

Once I had wrecked my firs░ car that was given to me for passing my test, after a few months I got another car, a fiesta. Not as fast as my other car for obvious reasons. It was my nan and grandad who decided they would buy me a car again, bless them both always – my nan is still with us, thankfully and we are still very close. But should they have bought me the car? Was I trustworthy enough on the road? The answer in one word… NO!

This is a story that even turns my guts still. It was terrible. Okay, to start with, through the story we have learnt a little about crack cocaine and its effects. The high is just unbelievably out of this world but you are not with it for a few seconds at least, and the hit is the INSTANT that you blow out the smoke. Now this is what I used to do. I would pull up at Holy Cross Church off of Whitmore way, and it had a long, bent road leading up to the church and I would make sure I had everything I needed to build a pipe and so I would. I would put a massive stone (of crack) on the pipe, get a tune on the stereo in the right place to hear the 'drop' of the tune (usually either 'Eminem's Stan' or a garage tune, 'Right before my eyes') and I would suck this pipe up and hold it in. I would slam the car in reverse and face down the road then put my foot down, I would wait until I hit about 50mph and wait for the tune to drop with the baseline and then I would blow it out. Wow! Absolutely disgusting that I could have killed anyone at any time of doing it but shit, what a buzz! I always did it at night when that road was 'dead' (as I should have been) though that's not the point. One time I did it in the day and as I hit 50mph on the bend there was a mini-bus full of old people. I so nearly hit them head-on. I swerved and mounted the curb bursting both passenger-side tyres and ending up in the bush, then I had to get out of the car and act normal to a bunch of people all asking me why I was travelling at that speed on a blind corner. No, I didn't need this. I just said, "Sorry people, real tired, been working all night, was just off home to sleep. I better walk it, again, I am so sorry!" and I walked off rather quickly and left the scene of the accident. It was not reported as a near-crash to the police so they must have just thought I had clipped the curb and called RAC to recover the car (nothing suspicious). That was the last time I did that. I would say that was about the 20th odd time I had done it so I didn't do bad As I didn't crash or kill anyone (apart from doing something really, really bad by even doing it in the first place!). I didn't kill anyone. Nearly though. And I'm lucky they didn't report me out of all of them…nothing, thank fuck for that. Sometimes I used to do it with a mate in the car. Fucking hell! They would shit their pants every time, huh. It's really not clever people, I don't advise it, even if you want to die don't take others with you, you have no right. I was just a cunt. A selfish fucked up cunt!!!

So, whilst living in the slums called 'Ryedene' bedsits a new crew from Hackney moved in on the Basildon patch obviously hearing that there was an opening in the market (as there always is unless a crew has a hold). Fucking hell, I was getting déjà vu, so, the first time I scored crack and heroin from these black boys I used the name Fisher. When I met them behind Stacey's corner shops for the first time they said they had been asking people after me as they had been told back in Hackney that I would link them up or be able to help with the new business in some way, as I knew all the smackheads or as they referred to them as 'cats'. Apparently, I was the man to see if you wanted to sell heroin or crack in the area you look for 'Fisher' (not a nice title to hold). Was I up for it all again? Yeah, fuck it…

So a Somalian fella, who called himself Jacob, asked me if I could help him in any way get him up and running and fast. I told him I not only knew 90% of the addicts but I got on with most of them too and if I told them to use a certain dealer you could put money on it that they would. Jacob asked if I could drive? and if I had my own place? I gave him the answers he wanted to hear – yes, I have a licence and yeah, I got my own place. I know he wanted a safehouse so how was I going to use this to my advantage? Because I didn't do anything for nothing. I wasn't in a position to. So I jumped in the motor with these two black fella's I had only just met and took them to my flat. We spoke for hours while Jacob plied me with crack cocaine, as much as I wanted. In three hours I would say I smoked about £300 worth whilst chatting, if not more. He also left me and my girlfriend a few balls of 'brown' (heroin) to smoke that evening. So, it was now set, Jacob would come from Hackney to my flat in Basildon every morning at nine o'clock spot on in a different motor each day. They used to call my area 'country', and when they were in their area they would call it 'the roads'. I thought this was strange as Basildon is hardly fucking country now, is it? It's a concrete shit hole!

Anyway, we would bag up £4,000 of crack and £4,000 of heroin to sell in one day (that's 400 wraps all in all), it sounds a lot but that on a good day would be gone by one o'clock (sometimes even earlier). That was the profit of £4,000 a day! Give or take because Jacob used to do some of the regulars 'deals' like two £20 balls for £30 and things like that so it was never a consistent amount of money there which helped me pull off a scam for 'perks'. When you wrap balls of crack and smack, you wrap them in such a way that you end up with about 40 to 50 little £20 balls on a carrier bag. So I would cut off all of them, barring a few, then I would throw the bag straight into the rubbish when no one was looking at me. On average, I was taking four £20 balls of both brown and white every morning for a very long time. That's £160 of gear a day that's without my payment for driving and use of my bedsit, which if I remember right was two white and a brown. I was fucking having it off mate! Once again, I was playing a dangerous game with bigtime drug dealers/killers who I didn't even know, their bosses were cartels and I was nothing to them, completely disposable. I know that now obviously and don't think I was always naive to this either. It's just that the drugs tend to cloud your judgment somewhat and you have no fear when on heroin.

At the time, I know I was mugging them off but I felt like part of Jacob's gang. His boss was named Marlon 'pretty boy', which they also named me. I met him a few times when the boys were finding their way, but once they had found me, it was passed over to Jacob and I. Jacob came down to mine one morning with a story that Marlon 'pretty boy's' best mate had had his head blown clean off with a double-barrel shotgun. They were in a feud which involved Hackney and Tottenham – they were literally at war. One night, 'pretty boy' was sitting in the passenger side of his best mate's BMW and a motorbike pulled beside them at the traffic lights and the bloke whipped out the sawn-off shotgun and took Marlon's mate's face/head clean off with it covering Marlon with his best mate's brains, LITERALLY, and this still didn't ring the alarm bells that it should have to keep me away. Instead, I got more involved and I know now even if we had just been pulled by the old bill on any of the hundreds of days I drove Jacob around if he had dropped the gear (100's of wraps of class A's), I would still be in prison now probably. I think he is.

I didn't even think of the risks; I was too caught up in the drugs and money and also clothing and Macdonald's and pub lunches with a pint etc at a time when I had nothing... I mean, this bloke I had only just met could see I was on my arse. He was taking me down to JD sports in Basildon town centre and buying me an outfit every day for a couple of weeks. I wasn't used to having so many changes of clothes these days being a heroin addict as all my money now days went on crack and smack for me and Carisa. The days of looking smart were behind me. Jacob was 'buying me'. I had no one apart from Carisa so I let him, no, not like that! He was even buying me outfits for the summer. He thought I was his 'bitch' but I knew what I was doing mate, I'm far from stupid. He was feeding a habit for two people without knowing it. I had already obtained this habit before even meeting him. I had a number of people after me, obviously, for all the things I had done to dealers, and one night, a friend of mine who lived a few doors away and who's place I used to be in a lot, had his door kicked off by a white fella and two black guys. They were asking for me but he kept his mouth shut so they chopped him in the shoulder with an axe nearly taking his arm clean off. I just remember looking out of my window early hours of the morning (around about 1 am) and the car park was lit up like a disco with blue lights, only at this gathering somebody was losing an arm. It wasn't a party. I wouldn't go so far as to say we were best mates or anything, but one of my mates had just been done with an axe and could lose his arm. Because of me! Shit, I felt terrible! Well… sort of. He was only a little mixed-race fella, he was not a fighter. If they had come through the right door I had taken the fucking axe off them and cut their fucking heads off. Anyway, this was almost the last straw. Jacob had been serving up from mine for ages now and I wanted out. He was bringing too much 'heat'. He was keeping a closer eye on things now too and so I wasn't even getting my perks anymore. I'd had enough and dangerous people were looking for me and getting closer all the time. One bloke even put three bullet holes in the side of Jacob's car as he passed in broad daylight outside mine because he thought I was in it. That's all I'll say on that as the fella in question is massively dangerous(still). So…the straw that broke the camel's back was this…

One day, Jacob wasn't about for whatever reason they didn't have any gear, me and a so-called good friend of mine, appropriately named 'psycho G', I mean this geezer was absolutely fucking off the charts nutty, was in a car once wanted. A copper spotted him and stood out on the road and ordered him to stop. 'G' instead put his foot down and mowed the copper down in the car knocking him 15ft in the air and driving off. He was then spotted somewhere in London by metropolitan police and they ran him over snapping his collar bone. I mean it was nearly coming through his skin and he still did a runner and got away. I see him walking around like that for about a month before he eventually went to the

148

hospital but was again arrested and released on bail. Eventually, he was caught after skipping bail once again and put away, but he was always in and out of prison it was second nature to him, like a home from home, literally. I even bought pills and acid trips from his wife on occasions before the heroin days that were upon us now. She hated what we did but she would still have a cheeky crack pipe from time to time.

Anyway, we were at my place and started to feel the pains kicking in from the cold turkey, we needed heroin but we had no money so what were we to do? 'Psycho G' told me a geezer we knew called B was picking up at three o'clock, a massive amount, so he said to me, "Why don't we just rob him?"

I think I pondered on it for about ten seconds before I felt the stomach and leg cramps getting worse along with the anxiety in my legs (restless leg syndrome 'extreme') kicking in therefore becoming agitated and restless. I decided, 'fuck it'.

I said to 'G', "Okay, fuck it, let's do it."

This guy 'B' lived about a 45-minute walk from mine but when you are clucking for heroin every single step you take feels like somebody is punching you in the stomach and kicking you in the back of the legs, its agony just to walk. So we took it easy and had a slow walk whilst deciding how we were going to do this! There was no real plan just simply turn up at the door and 'G' would knock as this B fella knew him. So when he opened the door, we would run in screaming like fucking maniacs in the hope we can scare B into handing over his drugs, I had done this before as you know. As we approached the area, my heart was in my mouth. I hadn't done this in a while and never with just two of us alone and with no fucking tools. What if the place is full of fucking big geezers all tooled up? Fuck it, what will be will be! I need this gear.

So, we got to his turning and tried to 'clock' the place for about an hour to see if there was any movement and who was in there. There was very little movement which was unusual for a dealer's house and usually meant they were dry (out of gear). This was not a good sign but we had walked all the way there and were now in a lot of pain withdrawing from heroin. So we approached the brown wooden panel door. The plan had quickly changed. I told 'G'. We had to do this quick, it was broad daylight. I kicked out one of the panels as hard as I could to make sure it went with the first kick otherwise they would obviously know we were coming. It went through. I bent down and reached through to open the door. We ran in there like a pair of fucking nutty animals screaming. Psycho G pulled out a used needle and threatened B with it. He handed over one £20 wrap of heroin (at the time I didn't know this) as soon as I saw something be passed I screamed, "Let's get the fuck out of here now!"

G was screaming at B saying, "Where's the fucking rest?"

I shouted, "Don't get fucking greedy, let's go!" We ran as fast as we could from there in case one of the neighbours had seen us do it. We were in agony by now. I just couldn't wait to get home and smoke some gear to feel normal again or at least just out of pain. I was asking G all the fucking way home, how much did we get? But he was being shady and not answering me. We got back to mine and G broke the bad news that we only had one ball of heroin between us worth twenty pounds. He didn't think to mention it all the way home despite me repeatedly asking him, "What did he chuck you, G?"

G looked at me, I was sat on the end of my bed and he was sat on the sofa. All of a sudden he pulled a needle in a packet out of his pocket and chucked it into my lap. He said, "Bruv, if you do it this way you'll be ok until tomorrow sometime. If I give you a bit to smoke, you'll be clucking again soon, I ain't really got enough."

I remember I sat with this packet in my hands for about three minutes actually considering it until all of a sudden I dropped it and to this day it still plays in my mind as if straight out of a film, I remember dropping the needle in its packet and it fell to the floor in super slow motion, with an almighty bang as it hit the floor, it will stick with me for as long as I live. The second the needle hit the floor I jumped up and I hit the fucking roof and I screamed, "Get the fuck out of my place, you fucking horrible cunt. You're supposed to be my mate and you're trying to get me to do that when I've never done it once. You are one lucky boy I don't go fucking sick on you right now and cut you to fucking bits, you good for nothing prick. You better fucking get out now, YOU CUNT!"

Only a real lowlife scumbag would do that and try and entice you into using a needle When I first ever realised it was heroin I was on, I made a promise to my deceased twin brother (who is and always has been my guardian angel) that if I ever use a needle, I would put enough in it to kill me so that I couldn't become a pinhead(someone that uses needles). But now, the thought of going to the lowest of the low had actually crossed my mind like never before. Now was the time! I wanted out of it all and I needed help. Now this was the last straw so I went to my mum's house and knocked on the door. When she opened it, I just fell to my knees crying and asking her to please help me but she was used to this and was waiting for the help that I wanted, to be money related for more heroin. I told her that I was ready. She said the first step was to talk to my granddad, who was the head of the family, and explain to him why this time would be different from all the others. As I had called out for this time and time again, he would want to know what was different this time to warrant the help I wanted, which was £8000 worth of implants I had heard about the stars and wealthy people having and that it was working for some, this was worth a shot. This is an implant called naltrexone and is designed to stop the effects of opiates working on the brain so that as much as you take it will not affect you in any way but there was also always a danger as you were at risk of overdosing without knowing it resulting in possible death. To have this implant, you first need to be free of heroin and all opiates for seven days which is the hardest part of the entire affair. As I have said before, they don't call it 'Lady H' for no reason. She's your mistress and you want her there forever by your side for you to lean on for everything. I knew I could not get clean in the flat I was in and I also knew it was not going to be easy to get free from Jacob and his crew as they were now based at my bedsit. I hatched a plan with my mum. It didn't take much thinking as I knew what I had to say to the council, exactly how I felt. I was also a registered heroin addict which puts you at the top of the priority in the housing by the council. Wrongly or rightly I was going to use this to my advantage!

I asked my mum in a polite manner to please help fund my habit for a couple of days just to free myself from Jacob by not opening the door, but I knew I couldn't get away with that for more than two or so days. So I went to the council offices first thing in the morning. I saw a friend of mine, Ben and his pregnant girlfriend. Now before carrying on, just to give you an idea, they were there for housing too and I got a place six months before them for being a heroin addict and they were PREGNANT. I told the people in there that I had heroin dealers and murderers working from my place and if I tried going to the police for help they would have me killed so the only option I was left with was suicide, and I went on to tell them all about my neighbour that had been chopped up as he was mistaken for me.

"If I'm not moved in the next two days, I'll kill myself," I said. This worked, they gave me the keys after a few days to another property, a 45-minute walk or ten-minute drive away at the opposite end of Basildon in Laindon. It had worked! I was a partway free Now for the physical addiction, oh, and the question… 'why are all big dealers on me to work with them all the time, and how am I going to get out of the criminal life, if not forever then at least for a while?'

My grandad was there to make sure I did not leave the flat and I had such bad pain in my legs I was punching them literally until they were black and blue just to try and numb them a bit to stop the aching and the anxiety feeling you get in your legs (restlessness). I even screamed at my grandad to get me a knife so I could hack off my own legs clean off and I meant it. This was hell!

This really is a life experience that you simply cannot put into words, or even given a week you couldn't explain it, it's the most painful and mentally destroying part of my entire life (nearly). My poor granddad, who has sadly passed now, had never seen or even heard of anything like this. It was completely alien to him. I will never forget when I was screaming out for a knife and punching myself until I was out of breath he looked over at me from the leather armchair opposite me and put his head in his hands and cried saying, "I just can't believe what this stuff has done to you!"

I had NEVER seen my grandad cry EVER! This stuff really affects the whole family, not just the user.

So, what I remember, on day one, I awoke knowing that today would be my first day without heroin in as long as I could remember. As you can imagine, this in itself causes anxiety and a slight sense of panic. Also you feel like there is something missing from your everyday routine that has been there for so long (in some, or most, cases, so many years). The first day there is no real pain as you probably still have a bit in your system from the night before but you have a certain 'anxiety feeling' in your arms and your legs that you just cannot explain. It causes you to need to keep moving them at all cost even if you are trying to stay still and as the day progresses, this will change, in most cases for the worse, but first, you miss the 'chase, normally for the money primarily and then the hunt for the 'gear', it all becomes routine. Normality! Though it really is not, surely. So boredom sets in pretty quickly which in turn caused me to get agitated pretty fucking quickly too. After a few hours (by mid-day), I'm pacing the flat with a runny nose, constantly sniffing and starting to get the shakes, also for some reason that I don't know, you start to yawn a lot and sneeze too, this is the onset of something fucking massive and really a painful route. Now I am thinking, *What have I done here? I have called it on! I am doing this! There is no going back this time*! and I am thinking, *How am I going to sleep tonight and how much pain am I going to be in for the next week? Can I do this?*

I am thinking all of this and it has only been a few hours of the very first day, and all I want to do is fucking kill someone or score some smack! The next couple of days would see me in such a way that pacing the flat had become a distant hope. I couldn't even fucking walk. I was crawling to the bathroom on all fours to go to the toilet and I was being sick in a bucket next to my bed. The pain in every single muscle in my body were screaming out in agony, in turn, causing me to scream out literally too. I wanted to die. Or I needed some heroin and I use the word 'needed' because I had truly had enough and no longer 'wanted' to be 'a smackhead'. I wanted my life back, though I did wonder what that life would consist of without 'Lady heroin' in it. I knew that it MUST be better than what I was living through ('groundhog day').

I had not gone 48 hours without heroin in at least four years now, my body was in shock in a massive way. I was sweating bucket loads but I was wrapping myself in blankets on my bed as I felt freezing cold. Then I would feel hot within minutes and so I was fighting to get out of them and kicking them off in angry rages with what very little strength that I had. This went on for hours, and then days, at one point, I wanted to lay on the fucking ceiling for no reason at all.

I felt like there was no end to this. I thought the pains and the sickness would never ever end. *I need heroin! I cannot take any fucking more! But...I'm half-way there now! If I smoke one line of smack now I go back to square one and I have to start the seven-day process of pure agony all over again. What do I do? I have got to continue I think.... I think I can do this.* At least deep inside I think I can because on the outside I was begging for gear, on my knees, eyes streaming and dribbling as I am screaming, "Please, just let me out for half an hour and I'll come straight back."

I wasn't lying I would have only been half hour and I would have been back. But, I would have been smacked up and as I said before 'back to square one', which meant the pain that I had already gone through so far would of all been for nothing. This was a mindset I had to now keep following and drum into myself. I was seeing it by day five that I was over the hill and nearly there. Though I had a long, long path ahead of me and I was still in absolute agony. One thing I hadn't even thought of yet How was I going to STAY CLEAN? If I even made the seven days. Well, there was one way I had heard of, Naltrexone implants. But you must be clear of all opiates (including methadone 'the heroin substitute') before they can operate and give you one of these implants. Hence the week from hell and the massive life change that is necessary first.

It was my grandad that was to pay for me to have the implants for two years costing around £8000. The professionals in the field say if you stay clean for two whole years your body and mind are completely clear of it all and the chances of staying clean are increased massively (by about 80%) I think, but I had to get through the seven days first.

If this book makes money, I promise to help as many heroin addicts as I can, with the right help that they need – counselling and implants; that would be my dream!!!

The first day was bad but just in my head really, well, a lot of it but the second day was when I was hitting myself and screaming. This was to get worse. Days three, four and five are an absolute killer; you will do anything for that gear. You need it, your body is crying out for it, you are being sick at the

156

same time as shitting yourself and this is NO exaggeration. Luckily my toilet was next to my sink so I was sitting on the loo with my head in the sink whilst all sorts were coming from both ends at the same time. I was sweating yet I was freezing cold as I said before. I would put my dressing gown on and within seconds I would be taking it off again and then a few minutes and it's on again. I was climbing the walls. I didn't see a vision of a dead baby on the ceiling but I did certainly contemplate suicide by hanging myself if I was left alone for long enough. Luckily, I wasn't, otherwise, I definitely would not be here now after escaping death time and time again before this 'in my eyes' would have been a waste. I wouldn't be able to tell this story right now. I even had a 100ml bottle of methadone in the fridge. Just a tiny sip like 10ml would have stopped the pure agony I was going through but again would have taken me back to square one. At the start, my mum said to me, "You need to get that out of there."

I said, "NO, I'm keeping it there so I know I have got the will power to really stop this and prove to MYSELF that now I was ready to turn my back on my mistress named 'Lady H' (heroin) forever!"

I kept it there until the end and then I tipped it down the sink on day seven. It felt like heaven, I felt so fresh and clean and also more 'with it' in the head. I managed to bath myself properly and get dressed up for a pub lunch with the family. Even though the surveillance had stopped, I was not allowed out without one of my family and deep inside I knew this was for the best. I only had to bump into Mark Richie and I would be practically forced into it. At that point of recovery, you are weak and vulnerable and easily lead back to it in an instant. After I had been through the hardest week of my life EVER I was to go for a meeting with a private doctor who specialised in implants to keep you from doing heroin. The meeting went well though I was a bit creeped out when he touched the area the implants would be put in (my lower abdomen under my belt line near my privates, my pubic area). I didn't like this due to past experiences that didn't surface until I was about 25 years old.

I remember my first implant appointment. I was shitting myself. I was even close to tears. I didn't know what to expect. I got there and was waiting for about half an hour. It felt like days were passing, I was so anxious. I was called into the theatre and sat on the bed where I would be being cut open at a site of my choice (either my arm or my lower abdomen) and having this implant put in me. Now, this was just an experimental drug from America. Not a lot of research had been done on it and so I had to basically signed my life away by signing a piece of paper saying that if I had a bad reaction to the implant and was TO DIE there would be no one to blame basically and also that if I was to take heroin whilst having the implant inside me it could kill me (this bit I understood). The idea of the implant is so that when you take heroin it has no effect on you whatsoever no matter how many times you try, but as you can imagine, this did lead to more than a few overdoses where people were trying to get high with the implant inside them and because the heroin didn't seem to be working, they would just take more and more of it and obviously end up killing themselves by overdosing. These are the people you could never help and didn't really want to be clean whereas I did and so many do. So, I laid back on the bed after signing the paperwork without even being given time to read it all, and I watched every movement the doctor made even down to the six injections to numb the area and then the scalpel puncturing my skin and slicing really deep into my lower abdomen. I was told time and time again to not watch but I said, "You know what? I want to watch this hell I have to go through because I want to remember to never go back to that drug."

But would it be the answer? would I stay clean? The very deep slice was made in my lower abdomen and a tube containing six little white balls (one for each month) a bit shorter than a cigarette but about twice the thickness was forced into the hole that they had made. It wasn't pleasant to watch or to feel. The force and the pressure used by the surgeon's finger to get it in was immense. The geezer had half his finger in me to push the implant right in. This would only last six months too and then I would have to come back and have this done another three times to cover the two years that the professionals advise you stay clean for, to make the journey that bit more likely to end up a success. Would it work for me? I was willing to give anything a go and I had heard of certain famous people having had it done and it was a success. What really gets me is, a famous figure or celebrity gets off of heroin and they are wonderful and an inspiration to others. I get off heroin and all I hear is, 'once a smackhead always a smackhead, he'll never stay clean'. Nah? Fucking watch me!

About a year later, it was a bright beautiful day, the sun was ablaze, it was 80 degrees Fahrenheit, and when I woke up that day, the last thing on my mind was the fact that I was to DIE TODAY. LITERALLY. I was back at work, I was clean still and I had bought a brand-new Renault Clio on finance. It was a £12,000 car and had never been driven apart from a test drive, it had eight miles on the clock. I had the car a few weeks and noticed something just was not quite right. One day pulling out from the owl and pussycat shops in Basildon, I revved up the engine and let the clutch go and the drive shaft fell out of the car and hit the floor beneath me. I had to have it towed and repaired. About a week later, I took it to the dealers in Laindon where I lived, I told them AGAIN I wasn't happy with the way the car was driving as when I was braking hard and it was kind of shuddering and shaking a bit and also pulling to the left but I needed the car back before the day after next as I had to get to work. So I went back at the end of the day to be told that there were three minor faults and one major fault but as I needed the car for work, coupled with the fact that they didn't have the parts, they told me to take the car and bring it back in a week. It was about three days after that, and as I said, a beautiful day. I went round to my mate Allan's parents' house to pick him up for a day out cruising to loud music in a nice motor (for my age and for only just being clean) looking for potential dates and phone numbers from any girls we should come across. Little did I know, today would become fatal. How I am still here to tell this 'mostly' true story is thanks to an amazing paramedic who I'll never have the chance to thank, and what I believe to be my twin brother in spirit looking over me.

I had just picked Allan up from his mum and dad's. It was mid-morning and the air was filled with the smell of fresh-cut grass as we were driving down Cranes farm road in Basildon past the playing fields that backed onto my mum's house (coincidently). The music was pumping and spirits between me and Al were high, to say the least. *It's the way* by DJ Marky was playing from the CD player through two giant house speakers I had wired up and thrown into the boot of the car as a makeshift system. We passed two young girls that I knew, well, one of which was named Alison who I had recently finished with just through boredom as she was a bit younger than me, the other, the younger sister of a very good friend of mine 'Greeny'. As I see them, I decided, stupidly, I would show off so put my foot down and speeded up only to about 70 mph in a 60 zone. I saw the massive roundabout that I was well used to taking at high speed, but today would be different. I slowed to 55 and went to take the roundabout. I steered to the left and as I pulled it back to the right to go around the roundabout, I heard an almighty bang from under the car and in the blink of an eye, the road beneath me was coming at my face. I remember screaming the word, "NO." The next big bang I heard was my last. I was not only unconscious but dead in the road and as I wasn't wearing a seatbelt, I had been catapulted from the car through the sunroof as it flipped into the air. The car apparently from eyewitnesses flipped forwards, bonnet first six times before finishing on its roof with Allan still in it. The ambulance, I heard, arrived very promptly and the two girls I knew were on the scene too and had called my mother to tell her. My mum had known something was up with me as soon as she heard the sirens out the back of her house. She says she automatically knew it was me. The paramedics were just about to pump me full of morphine (the same substance as HEROIN) once stabilizing my body and resuscitating me too to start me off breathing again, but Alison just in time shouted, "He has a tag around his neck."

I had a tag that said because of the naltrexone implants, I had to stop me doing heroin, I wasn't allowed anything opiate or adrenaline based. It could kill me instantly! So it was a bloody good job she intervened considering I had just been clinically dead on the scene and saved already once. One of my best friends at the time came down the road the other way and saw the police everywhere with the road closed on the other side and the car on its roof. My mate said to his missus, "That's Fishers motor."

His Mrs said, "Don't say that," but Ben recognised all my tools in the road for tiling and a basketball that I had on the parcel shelf. I was rushed to Basildon hospital where my mother was told that there had been a car crash and the driver was dead. She fell apart there and then, but they had it wrong, and then I woke up, about forty-five minutes later, still in a pool of blood and to my family and two police officers stood in front of me with a breath tester for alcohol. As I looked down, I was having my most expensive clothes I had cut off of me by the emergency doctors. I must have been in shock as all I was concerned about was my two-tone black and silver jeans and my Moschino shirt as opposed to the fact that my head was in a pool of blood. The whole top half of the bed was blood-soaked but I was in no pain. I had lost all the skin and flesh from my right hand which I had used to protect my face after the first bang of the crash as soon as I saw the road coming at me from beneath. You could literally see the veins and bones in my hand when unwrapped. However, this scarring could have been my face forever. My hand and wrist were broken but could not be operated on at the time due to the risk of infection as it was an open wound. It would take months to heal and would be permanently noticeably disfigured, or so I was told. Also, this meant the bones inside would heal wrong, so I would have to go back at a later date and have it broken, reset and pinned. The police said, "Sorry mate we know you're going through hell right now but this has to be done, Sorry."

I did the breath test and passed as I had not had a drop of alcohol. I didn't drink and drive although I took other things and drove at times (like a dick head!) but now I was clean. I hadn't had any drugs though. The police then said to me, "Also we would be nicking you for not wearing a seatbelt but we believe that if you had your belt on you would never have survived this terrible accident as the roof was caved in to the seats headrest."

They went on to tell me they had three independent women witnesses to say I was not speeding or driving in any dangerous manor. They also went on to quiz me about a third person who was seen leaning over my body and was watched as he casually walked off into the bushes. There was no third person!!!

The description fitted me! Make of it what you will. I know what I've been told by a medium and I know what I believe. The twin brother I used to see in the mirror when I was four years old was there to save me and save me he had. I had suffered such a blow to the back of my head that it opened up seven inches long and has left a patch where hair will not grow now, it's a nasty scar. A reminder not to take life for granted and try to live every day exactly how I want to and enjoy myself whether that be smoking a joint, drinking a beer, or at night time this, writing!!!

Also, my hip ball and socket joint had dislocated but on the impact of bouncing along the tarmacked road had smashed back into place which then bruised between the bones and they said I would be laid up in hospital for a couple of weeks. So being me, I stayed one night and discharged myself to go home. Well, I had to say I was going back to my mum's but I didn't. So, what happened to Allan? Well, he had his belt on but the roof didn't cave his side luckily, but he did snap both wrists and was awake through the whole thing which left him traumatised. Now, I heard Allan was having a claim up against me for the accident and was laying it on real thick to get as much as he possibly could. I also heard that because he was in the process of the claim against me he would not step foot out of his house through fear that he would bump into me and if I knew about it I would bash him. He was wrong, I completely understood. Look my insurance was going to skyrocket after this accident anyway for sure, so what was his claim going to do? It was not going to make any difference to me, so I went round to his mum and dad's house and knocked and asked for Al. At first, they said he wasn't in but somehow I didn't think that Allan's parents were into garage music and MC'ing so I said, "Look, do me a favour, I ain't here for trouble otherwise I wouldn't waste my time using the letterbox to knock now, would I? Just get Allan to the door please!"

Allan came to the door in his dressing-gown acting all sheepish and weary. I said to him, "Look mate, I hear you're having a claim up man? It doesn't make a blind bit of difference to me pal, you go ahead and don't feel bad bruv. Honest, it's cool, just sort me out a drink eh!"

Anyway, he invited me in and his parents thanked me for coming round and putting his mind to rest as he hadn't been out in weeks through fear of bumping into me and getting a beating. It was his dad that was pushing for the claim obviously as Al was too young but I initially heard Allan got £17,000 compensation but I have recently heard that he got A

164

LOT more than that. I have never heard a word from him since.

Yeah, cheers MATE! Little fucker didn't even think to sort me out a grand (£1000), tight! If I ever see him again, I probably would give the fat fuck a slap just for being a tight cunt. After the bad crash, I got another Clio on the insurance this time a different (limited edition) colour and I had all the windows blacked out, it looked the bollox. I'm driving back to my flat in Laindon from Macdonald's and I get a phone call on my mobile and it's my mate, Ben. He said to me, "Fisher fucking hell man, Ross needs help, he's tried killing himself a few days ago and was found face down in a road somewhere by an ambulance. All because the girl he was in love with had cheated on him."

I said to Ben, "Right bruv, I'm going straight round there now."

So I turned around at the next roundabout and headed straight for Ross' place on Craylands estate. I got out the car and put my shades on; I was dressed smart as always once again, and I climbed the stairs to Ross' mum's maisonette and banged on the door. It took a while to get an answer but the second I shouted through the letterbox, "Its Fisher, bruv. Open up," the door was open in seconds. Ross seemed so excited to see me. I don't know how long it had been but it had been a while. Anyway, his spirits seemed higher for seeing me than I expected. So, I said to Ross, "Right, get showered, open all the curtains, put some tunes on. Here I got a CD here, garage bruv, whack it on! I'm taking you out right now so hurry up!"

I had a pocket full of cash and a £12,000 brand new motor. I was going to show him that there are plenty more fish in the sea. All you gotta do is go fishing. I don't mean literally for those who are a bit slower than most. Ross jumped in the shower, got ready and off we went out into the sunshine for the day. First stop, cashpoint. Next stop, anywhere we could see girls. We just drove around all day pulling over and chatting up different groups of girls in their flash motors. At one time, I said to Ross, "Watch this! This is how easy it is."

I drove for about two minutes before I spotted a small group of teenage girls and I pulled over and simply shouted out, "Oi, gis ya number! Yeah you, ya number!"

One girl broke away from the crowd and came over to the car and put her number in my phone. I said, "Cheers, I'll bell ya," and I simply drove off. I said to Ross, "Look that's how easy it is, so don't be killing yourself over one girl, you WILL ALWAYS meet someone else in time bruv, ALWAYS, you get me?"

He tells me to this day that that day saved his life and helped him see that there was more out there and plenty more women to date and with a friend like me, (who would put my life on the line for him) there was no need to be down. I would always be there to pull him out of any bad situation he may find himself in and I still am here for him like a brother. I always will be. As I know he is for me too. I even got him a job as a youngster with me and Colin tiling. He was just loading out tiles and grouting for us but it was cash in his pocket for the weekend. For quite some time he was working with us and I spent most evenings with him and two girls of my choosing for the evening and then every weekend in the car gathering girls' phone numbers for the week ahead. He still says I changed his direction in life and he says he wouldn't be here if it wasn't for me! *Love you, brother!*

One day, me and Ross went to a flat where a Jamaican Yardi called 'Spesh' lived. He lived with a girl I'd known since infant school so I thought I was safe. We were after a bit of crack cocaine, (I was still clean from the heroin but dabbling in coke and crack) we were spending thousands on it a week at the time. I didn't know what I was walking into but I was well used to it by now and I didn't really give a fuck. I'd learnt their Yardi slang and 'patois' from hanging around with the (Love or Money) gang. We were there about half-hour whilst 'Spesh' got on the phone. After telling me he'd run right out, we were gutted and just wanted some gear. 'Spesh' asked me if I'd drive to London and pick up an amount to reload him.

I said, "Yeah, no worries, whatever."

So he got back on the phone and started talking Yardi slang, I clocked straight away he asked the fella on the other end of the phone to plot us up and take my brand spanking new car off me and just kill me and Ross and just leave us in an alleyway somewhere, we were going to get shot. I got on the phone to my mother and said, "What mum... Really? I'll be straight round give me two minutes."

I told 'Spesh' I had a family emergency and we had to leave, it was a fucking lucky escape AGAIN. Proper close call. Ross wanted to go back there tooled up and smash him and his mate up, but I talked him out of it. Ross would kill for me and the same favour would be returned at any time. We are still the same for each other to this day, 21 years later! He's in jail right now (2017) and as I'm finishing this story (2021) he is inside too but when he's out, we have work to do. Unless this book gets me out of trouble then I can forget about the issues I have going on now and just move on. Now THAT would be a dramatic change to my life, and pretty ironic to make money from something legal after spending my life committing crime to earn money and getting nowhere fast. Kids…IT DON'T WORK!!!

Problems with the Yardies were becoming a theme. I awoke one morning and I had about £80 enough for four white (Four £20 balls of crack). I called a Yardi that I knew well and had dealt with for years named Marsh. This fella was a real character but also ran a gang of stone-cold fucking Yardi killers. He was a tiny little black bloke with dreadlocks past his waist and a real swagger as he walked. He had a stutter so bad many people couldn't understand him. This is how he spoke and I am NOT exaggerating. I'd call him and this is how the conversation would go:

"Yo Marsh, it's Scott. Can I get four white?"

"Hey Scat, m m m m m m m m m m m m m m meet me at the the the the the the the the the the the shop five m m m m m m m m m m m m m minutes man."

I mean this fella could hardly talk, he was so cracked out of his face. Anyway, I went to meet him. When I got there 'Marshy' (as I called him) said to me (I won't put the stutter in), "Hey scat, (that's how he pronounced my name) do you know Scatt Fisher?"

I paused for a second to think and came out with, "Yeah, I know him quite well as it goes, why's that Marsh?"

He lifted his t-shirt up and showed me a stab wound in his lower abdomen! It had been stitched but it looked really bad. He went on to say, "Scat Fisher done this to me, do you know where he is? I have a crew out looking for him! He fucking called me to meet him and he stabbed me and robbed me, man. He's a fucking dead man walking!"

Alarm bells rung loud I said to Marsh, "Look, I'm Scott Fisher. That's me, Marsh!!!"

He went on to say that it was definitely Scott Fisher that did it and that there was another one. We went back and forth for ages as I tried to explain that there was only one Scott Fisher around Basildon and that was me. I told him that somebody had used my name as I was known to rob dealers, and I had my suspicions of who it was. Mark Richie, the very bloke that I hated, and if you remember, who got me on heroin without me knowing what it was. Scumbag! I repeatedly tried to tell 'Marshy' that it was Mark but he wasn't having any of it, so I just told him to make sure his boys didn't come for me. Fucking hell this is all I need. I didn't mind taking a beating if I had done something but this time I was truly innocent. Now I was on edge thinking that I might get jumped and stabbed by a group of Yardies in a case of mistaken identity. Fuck! Mark had dropped me in it BIG TIME and once again, it was a case of walking around looking over my shoulder AGAIN! I had got used to this, sadly.

So, I had been dropped off from work to the yard where my mum worked in the office, she was to give me a lift home. I can't remember why I was not on the road myself at the time, probably due to another car crash, as I have had about six. We left the yard in Wickford about 25 minutes from my flat in Laindon. My mobile phone rang, the screen said 'HOME!' I lived alone at the time and no girl was in my flat (for a change). So what the fuck is going on? I answered it by saying, "Who the fuck is this?"

A voice replied and said, "It's Paddy, mate, I came to knock for you and your door was wide open. Bruv, I think someone's robbed ya."

This fella was from Moss Side, Manchester, he was a fucking handful and a raging heroin addict. I said to him, "Does it look like anything's missing? My TV and my stereo?"

He said, "Mate, it looks like everything's here, it's just been messed up in here."

So I said to Paddy, "Stay where you are, I'll be ten minutes max."

He said, "Bruv, I was gonna wait for you anyway because they might be getting a van or something and come back for your stuff," acting as if he's helping me out. Anyway, I told my mum to put her foot down and I got back to the flat double lively. I had asked Paddy on the phone why the hell was he knocking for me as I was no longer on heroin and I was staying away from all that lot including him and I had also told them all to stay away from me too. I felt terrible turning my back on all the people I had been hanging around with for years but if you want to stay clean from that drug, it's what you must do. It's almost like the first day of school again as you now have to make new friends all over again and this time with clean people, but could I do it? So, back to Paddy and the flat. I arrived home. I jumped out of my mum's car and raced up the stairs to the top floor where I lived. The door was open and as I approached it, I see Paddy sitting on my sofa looking like nothing has happened. I ran into the flat and looked around. My bedside drawers were all over the floor and things had been messed up and thrown about but all my big stuff was there. It looked like nothing had been taken (an ex-girlfriend perhaps?). I said to Paddy, "Right, you can go now I don't want anything to do with you I've already told you that!" But Paddy was trying to get me to thank him for doing me a favour and waiting there to make sure they didn't come back. He said, "Ain't ya gonna thank me then?"

I turned to him and looked at him with an evil glare and said, "You have got five seconds to leave or I'll cut your fucking face off YOU CUNT."

I was not in the best of moods. I walked into the kitchen and grabbed a ten-inch knife turned around and looked at him again. He said, "Fine. Fuck you, I'm off," and he left sharpish. No pun intended. I knew something wasn't quite right. Paddy was one of the dodgiest blokes I knew and that is saying something. This was a Monday, the Friday before that weekend my grandad had given me a very expensive solid gold watch made by Claude Valentini. I wasn't used to wearing a watch and had forgotten all about it in the whirlwind that was going on. Yep, you've guessed it! The cunt had taken it, not only had he taken it but he had fucking mugged me off in a massive way. Standing face to face with me in MY flat and then asking me to thank him and all along he's got my watch in his fucking pocket... Wanker mate!!! But what goes around comes around and karma is a motherfucker, huh?

A few weeks passed and I bumped into Paddy and he asked me if he could have a word. So he said, "I hear you think I took your watch!"

I replied, "No Paddy, I don't THINK anything mate, I KNOW who took the watch," and I walked off leaving him wondering. About two days later, somebody burnt his mother's house down while she was out. To this day he thinks it was me but it wasn't, it was just a coincidence as this fella had a lot of enemies. I mean he made a new one every fucking day, so many people hated him and like I said karma is a bitch mate, this was poetic justice at its best. In my head, I got my own back in a funny sort of way as he thought it was me even though it wasn't.

Paddy called me a few weeks later and said, "I need to meet up with you, I've got something nice for you."

Now I had heard that line before and it spelt trouble. To put it bluntly, it normally meant you were going to get stabbed or shot. There was no way I was backing down though, so I went to meet him in my car. It was my second Renault Clio after the crash and I had all the windows tinted so dark that they were illegal but I didn't care. So I pulled up in a remote car park in Laindon where he had told me to meet him. I had never been to the place before. I was sitting there, it was late on a winter's night and it was foggy and drizzling with rain and what with my windows being so dark and the area being unlit I could hardly see a thing outside of the car and nobody could possibly see in. I was waiting for about ten minutes before I see a figure with its hood up approaching the car in the pissing down rain, it was Paddy. I unlocked the central locking and he climbed in. He started chatting just general shit like how have you been and what you been up to etc, and before I even got to say, "What the fuck do you really want?" one of my best mates to this day, 'Mr Ross Tappenden aka Rooster' (remember Ross?) leant over from the back seat where he had been hiding and reached into Paddy's half-open jacket and pulled out a massive ornamental solid metal blade. And shouted at Paddy, "What the fuck is this then, you cunt?"

Paddy didn't know Ross was in the back like that and he shit himself and said, "Aar, bruv, I got it for you because I know you love your knives and stuff. I thought it could go on your wall in your flat."

172

Now this thing wasn't sharp but it was fucking heavy, it had a lot of weight to it and if he had of reached into his coat and smashed me across the knees (like he was going to) I would be in a fucking wheelchair now. Having Ross hiding in the back was genius and once again, I had been saved and I put it down to that man Ross. No sooner had Ross got the blade, Paddy was out of the car. He didn't hang about after that which kind of says to me that he was going to do me with it. He seriously thinks I burnt his mum's house down and he wanted revenge. He didn't get it. I drove off in relief if I'm honest, not that I showed it. I was laughing and joking about it just as I had from so many situations, luckily.

People say that I'm like a cat and that I've got nine lives but I think I've used nearly all of them by now and if that's the case, then I could be using my last one writing this book. People are shutting me down on twitter right now for promoting this up and coming story of my life. Err, why? 'Love or Money' perhaps? I don't know!

I was clean off of heroin at this time and I decided to go out of for a meal over the festival leisure park to a pub with my mum and Colin and also my mum's best friend and her partner who looked like a little geeky looking fella but apparently, he was a martial arts expert/teacher and bloody good at it, a black belt in something or other. So, we're sitting waiting for our food and I clocked two blokes at the bar giving me the eye. Now I was very paranoid when I first got off of heroin, obviously, because of the life I lived, I was always looking over my shoulder or around the bars and restaurants for people I might have turned over as I no longer had the backing of 'Love or Money' they were all locked up.

I said to my mum, "Them fellas over there are going to kick off with me later."

My mum said, "Don't be silly, it's your paranoia don't worry," but I kept my eye on them all night I mean every single movement they made, I just had a bad feeling. Whilst we were there one of my old pals from before the heroin days that I had ripped off walked in. We called him 'Slick' (it was his DJ name) I won't disclose his real name as he is still an active criminal and is serving time behind bars at this present moment for shooting someone with a sawn-off shotgun. Anyway, I think I had knocked him for about £40 so I walked up to him and his crowd of friends and tapped him on the shoulder and said, "Alright bruv?"

He replied, "Alright? Are you taking the piss?"

I stopped him in his tracks talking and simply said, "Look bruv, I'm clean now, and here is a bullseye for your night! (£50) I'm getting on top, mate, sorry I was a wrong'n, apology accepted?"

He hugged me at the bar and said we were all good again. Still, I'm clocking these other two dickheads and they are glaring right at me and mumbling shit under their breath at me and sniggering. I turned and went back to join my family and friends at the table hoping Slick would hang around until we left for a bit of help as I didn't have a clue what these boys were 'holding' (meaning a gun or a knife perhaps). I said to my mum again that I thought the two plums were going to cause trouble but again, it was just put down to my heightened senses because of recently getting clean. So, we had the meal and dessert; it was lovely. As soon as we asked for the bill, the two dick heads both took turns to walk outside and stash their empty pint glasses. I knew then what was going to happen and I said to my mum, "Right, be ready, its gonna kick-off."

So we walked out of the doors of the pub and turned left to go round towards a long dark road that we had to walk down to get home. As we turned the corner, one of the blokes was taking a piss with his cock out in front of my mum and her mate, so I shouted at him, "Have some fucking decency and put it away, ya cunt."

He did. Then the next thing I know is he is coming at me with a pint glass in his hand and his arm raised as if he was going to do me in the face with it. I ducked quickly and pulled out CS gas and sprayed him in the face with it. I screamed at him, "Fucking run cunt while you can…NOW," and he turned and ran in zig-zag lines down the road as he couldn't see a thing.

He was screaming out like a fucking baby girl. I turned around and the bigger one out of the two was now coming at me with another glass to do me with. I waited for him to get close and I sprayed him too. He kept coming and just saying, "Is that all you've got?"

I didn't affect him at all. So as he threw the glass at my face once again I ducked in time and punched him hard on the chin. He went straight to the floor, so I turned and walked away thinking it was all finished. All of a sudden I heard my mum scream out, "LOOK, LOOK, it's Colin, look," as I turned the bloke was on the floor on top of Colin in the mud and rain, continuously punching him in the face. I was about twenty meters away and I turned and took a good run up and with shoes with a big metal buckle on the front of them and I kicked the bloke in the face as hard as I possibly could. He went from the position of being on top of Colin to the parallel

175

matrix position in the air as he flew off of Colin and into the road onto his back so I just kept kicking him. I looked up and there was a massive crew of doormen just standing still at the end of the road watching the fight go on. I kept kicking this bloke all around the road until I see the ambulance someone had called coming up the road, so I turned and left sharpish. As I stopped kicking him and started walking home towards where the doormen were, they all started to walk quickly towards me as if they were on their way to sort it (after I'd seen them stood still and watching).

One of them grabbed me, he was only a small fella he grabbed my shirt and said, "Think you better wait here."

I grabbed him by the chin and said to him angrily, "Look into my fucking eyes dick head! Do I look like I'm fucking staying here to you?"

He replied, "Look, just go quick, the police have been called."

so I did before the police got there. Just as I was leaving the complex I see about five police cars entering. I heard nothing of it ever again. So, what happened to the martial arts expert we were with? Well, he saw me go fucking mental and shit himself and stayed well out of it even though he was the first to see Colin getting done. It's not hard to work out who your friends are sometimes. Then again sometimes you do not work out who your friends are on time or even before they plot your murder. Talking of a murder being plotted, mine was. And this is what happened.

My friend Jim was running crack and smack to customers for a black fella named Leroy. There was another bloke there called 'Fat Man'. He was a big old lump and tried to be intimidating towards me but he didn't know me or what I was capable of or even what the fuck I had been through. So I just acted as if I didn't give a shit. I had about £80 on me and wages coming in two days' time. I was still staying well away from the heroin and I still had the implants in but I continued to smoke rocks (crack) for about a year or so. If anything, smoking crack helped me stay away from the heroin which most heroin addicts will wonder how on earth that's true as normally after you do crack for the massive high you then, in turn, need heroin to help you come down, but I didn't. I could have a crack session and just smoke a bit of weed after and I would be sort of with it again. So, me and Jim meet up at the big Q chip shop and he said to me, "Bruv, come with me for the night and I'll sort you out a few pipes (of crack)."

I also had a little bit of money so I thought, *Yeah, it could be a good evening.* So I went with Jim to his boss's house (Leroy's) and tonight would turn out to be the night my murder was planned!

I walked into the house and there were three black fellas I didn't know, except Leroy. He was from the city but using his grandma's house in Basildon to serve up from and he even had her locked in a bedroom by key from the outside so that she couldn't come out. I thought this was fucking disgusting but I kept my mouth shut as I had not yet worked this little crew out. I had a pipe in my pocket so I bought three £20 rocks from Leroy and asked him if I could smoke it in the house (out of respect). He and his mates roared out with laughter and said, "Yeah bruv, you can do what you want in here, just don't take the fucking piss ya know? And whatever is done or said in here fucking stays in here…okay?"

So I pulled out my pipe in an instant and set it up. I was shaking with anticipation and I felt like I needed a shit. This was something you will always feel just before taking the drug, as it's such a massive high. Anybody that does it or has done it will know what I am talking about 'the bubble guts'. so I did a pipe and oh wow, was it nice! I opened up immediately to these black fellas I had never met and I was wet from the walk as it was pissing down with rain outside and I said to Leroy, "Mate, you got a top I can borrow for the evening? No old shit though mate!"

He gave me a sky-blue Nike hoodie and told me he had bought it that day and not to ruin it. I said, "Of course not, bruv."

I didn't plan on getting it so blood-soaked from neck to waist so that it would be completely ruined and unfixable later that night. So, me, Jim, Leroy and his pals were all just floating about downstairs just in and out of the living room and kitchen but there were a few other fellas in a bedroom upstairs who I didn't clap eyes on all night. I was cracked up completely out of my nut. I don't exactly remember much about them next couple of hours that passed leading up to a very sobering moment that was to happen later, me and Jim were in and out of the house to different meeting points, meeting addicts and giving them heroin or crack for their money that they had probably spent the whole day trying to get or robbed from some poor bastard. I didn't like it but I was too buzzing to really care. I also went out in the car with 'Fat Man' to do a couple of drop offs. He seemed to want to get to know me (as all drug dealers seemed to). A call came through and Jim was the one to have to meet the fella on the other end. His name was Sean and he was bloody well known for robbing people (I mean this fella would have robbed his own nan, put her in a carrier bag and flogged her for a tenner to buy smack. And probably just stab her up after for fun. He was pure scum of the earth!

Anyway, Jim asked me if I would go with him and do the deal for him as he didn't want to get stabbed or robbed (yeah cheers, MATE). Stupidly, I agreed and went to a phone box to meet him. As we approached the phone box, there was a car sat there with about five people in it. We walked towards the car to do the deal. Sean jumped out of the car, now he is only a small fella but he loves to use a tool (weapon). He approached me and said, "It's Fisher, ain't it?"

I said, "Yeah, why?" and as I did he slipped out from his sleeve, a small rounders bat (like a mini baseball bat), grabbed hold of my hoodie that I was wearing (that I had borrowed from Leroy) and smashed me over the top of the head, opening up a wound so big the blood instantly ran into my left eye. I felt the blood running down the left side of my face instantly and fucking loads of it, it was gushing fast. I must have gone into shock instantly because I promise you I hardly felt a thing and I did not go down either. This angered Sean and so he hit me again in exactly the same place another TWO times. I still didn't go down and Jim was shouting, "RUN, RUN."

I said, "Fuck that, I ain't running from no one mate," then I looked Sean in the eye and just laughed and said, "Do you really think you'll get away with this? You cunt," and I spat blood at him, he let go of my hoodie and looked shocked that I was bleeding from the head due to three solid blows and I still didn't go to the floor like most people, I think you'll agree, would have. He grabbed the smack out of my hand and did a runner in the motor without paying, but I have got to say, I didn't put up much of a fight to keep it, to be honest. It was 60 quid's worth that I would now have to pay back to Leroy, simple. Instead of going straight to the hospital, I thought it best to go back to Leroy's nan's house and one, explain what had happened and two, and more importantly, I wanted more crack. We got back to the safe house (Leroy's nan's house) and everyone made a big fuss going on about the amount of blood that was pumping out of the top of my head and they all said that I should get straight to the hospital. I said, "Fuck all that, give me some more rocks, please mate, I'll pay for it!"

Jim gave me two rocks which are about ten pipes altogether, I started piping and they were all telling me my blood was pumping out quicker due to the rock sending blood to my head and making my heart and blood pump faster. How I didn't collapse, I don't know. I didn't care, but what was to happen next would…well…scare the shit out of me!

Leroy took a phone call and walked off into the other room, this was unusual and I pick up on everything from learning to study my surroundings and people's body language from a young age, and it's bloody lucky I do. He came back into the room after taking the call and his attitude and whole persona towards me was completely switched and he was giving me evil looks. He told me to take his hoodie off 'now!' So he could try and save it in the wash. He took the hoodie and walked into the kitchen to put it in the washing machine with half a bottle of vanish or something. He was being really off with me, I could sense it. As he came out of the kitchen through the living room towards the stairs through another door he walked past and give me a grin as he flicked a 4-inch butterfly knife around his hand in a style that I could see he was used to handling this blade. I see this and started to wonder what the fuck was going on. Oh well… Another pipe quick eh?

Jim looked across at me and said, "Bruv, I think you are in shit."

I just said, "Fuck it, I ain't done anything. I'll pay the £60 Sean robbed, no worries."

Then Leroy came back down the stairs where his other black friends were hanging out (separate to us for some reason). He came through the living room door and said to me, "I want you to go and take two balls of brown (smack) to 'Fat Man' at the garages, yeah?"

So I didn't think anything of it, I just thought 'Fat Man' was just meeting someone and he didn't have enough on him so I left the house and walk round to the garages to where he was parked in the dark unlit area I knew well. I jumped in the motor with this bloke I had only met recently tonight. I gave him the two balls but there was no one else there waiting for it or anything as I had expected. 'Fat Man' started up the car and started to drive slowly and staying completely silent not saying a word to me. I'm thinking, *Fucking hell, what have I done and what is going on?*

Anyway, he started to drive in the direction of the house I had just left. This was all very strange. I felt that something wasn't quite right. As we pulled up outside the house, 'Fat Man' pulled up outside and he looked at me and said, "Grab that bag from the back seat and bring it in but be careful with it!"

It was an old black 'Head' triangle-shaped holdall if you remember them. I got out of the car and opened the back door to get the bag and again 'Fat Man' said, "Make sure you're fucking careful with that."

I said, "okay." He knocked at the door one of the other black fellas I didn't know opened the door and let us in. As you opened Leroy's nan's door, you faced the stairs and on your immediate left was the living room door which then led on to the kitchen. So, we walked into the living room and 'Fat Man' said, "Put the bag there on the arm of the sofa and sit down."

So that's what I did. I didn't expect what was to come next. He opened the bag and pulled out a massive beach towel and started to unravel something which turned out to be a sawn-off shotgun. I looked around at my 'so-called' mate 'Jim' and he just put his head down and stayed quiet. 'Fat Man' rested the shotgun on my right kneecap and told me it was loaded and he could take my leg clean off with it with one pull of the trigger. He said to me, "We don't fucking do this shit for fuck all mate and we don't tolerate grasses!" this confused me.

I was absolutely petrified but I was not going to show it and I thought this was all a bit extreme over £60 worth of brown. I said to him, "Look mate, I ain't scared of that, or you, and you would get longer for pulling that trigger than you would for serving up a bit of gear! What the fuck?"

As he went to reply, Leroy came down the stairs and into the living room. As he saw what was going on, he shouted at the top of his voice to 'Fat Man', "Oi, I didn't tell you to get that fucking thing out. Put it away and get the fuck out of here now we don't need the noise!"

So he wrapped up the shotgun and put it back into the bag and left pretty quickly. Leroy still wasn't talking to me though. *What the fuck is going on here? Is it me, because I'm paranoid from piping? Everything seems weird! I don't like*

182

it! Leroy walked past me again and flashed the shiny butterfly knife and said to me, "We're gonna walk you around the garages in a bit mate. We'll walk you half-way home innit as you're bleeding so much." and then he went back upstairs to his pals.

This didn't make sense, why would they 'walk me home' or even half-way? There were more of them upstairs by now, I had heard them arrive. They were all on the pipe up there too. I had it in my head that they were going to stab me up 'obviously', much quieter than a gun in your nan's house, or on a housing estate eh?

I was sat by the window on the sofa and I was looking out and all of a sudden a brand spanking new white 5 series BMW with black tinted windows pulled up. The driver got out to open the back doors of the car for someone to get out. Then out stepped one girl. She was a black girl dressed in a white dress, then a massive black fella stepped out in an Armani suit with a white collarless shirt, followed by another girl. She was a white girl and dressed in the exactly the same dress as the black girl only in the opposite colour (black). *What was he some sort of fucking pimp?* He turned out to be 'the boss' and he had to have been called from London for something big. The two girls stepped through the door and into the living room as the big bloke just stepped in and went straight upstairs. Me and Jim stayed silent and just kept looking at each other like 'what the fuck?'

One of the girls (the white one) said, "which one of you is Fisher?"

I said, "Me, why?"

She turned to the black girl and almost broke down crying and started hyperventilating, saying things like "I don't want anything to do with this! This is really wrong, it's sick!"

It was then I put everything together and realised they were PLANNING MY MURDER!! They were going to walk me round to the pitch-black unlit garages and stab me quietly, it was so clear all of a sudden. My heart was in my mouth. I didn't know how I was going to get out of this. I stood up from the sofa and walked over to the door that lead to the front door on your right and the stairs on your left facing down to the front door. I looked and the keys were in the door. I looked up the stairs, to my left and there was about five of them if not more, all black fellas huddled around in a circle with their arms over each other's shoulders plotting something clearly. I quietly tried the door handle by reaching over but it was locked so I had to turn the keys (that were luckily left in the door) and I knew this was going to make a noise and alert them. I did it as quick as I could, fuck the noise, and I opened the door and I ran. I was in such a panic that I was trying to run so fast I kept falling face down on the pavement. It was as if my legs would not go as fast as my brain wanted them too. The top half of my body was trying to move quicker than my legs could carry it. It was like one of those nightmares where you run and run but you can't get away from whatever it is you are trying to escape and the fear is intense, only this was real, these boys wanted me dead! But why?

It was gone midnight and as I was running I was trying to get my phone out and call my mum to meet me and pick me up to first off, get me away from the area and, second of all, take me to the hospital to get my open head wound seen to. I managed to get my phone out whilst running and dropped it.

It hit the floor and the back came off and the battery came out, I had to stop. I think this was the first time I had actually looked back. There was no one following me thank the spirits that guard me. I managed to piece my phone back together and call my mum. I was completely out of breath and cracked up, I don't know what I said but I told her to pick me up at the petrol station which was closed on Whitmore way where I was hiding behind a sign, holding it still, (you know one of them metal ones that spin round in the wind) and that somebody was out to kill me. Within about five minutes, my mum was there and shocked at the amount of blood I was covered in. She rushed me straight to Basildon A&E where they gave me a few little numbing injections around the area before sowing it up. They wanted to keep me in because of the severe blows to the head but there was no way I was staying in there for the night so I told them my mother would be looking after me for the next 48 hours but as soon as we got outside I said, "Just drop me at the flat."

My mum wasn't happy but I've always been stubborn and do as I please, when I please, evidently, danger to my life or not. This was just another night in a day of my life that I had escaped almost certain death. So, remember the phone call Leroy took that started this all off? His name is Sean as I said, he had called Leroy and told him I was a police informant, WHICH I NEVER HAVE BEEN, and I am disgusted anyone would think I was.

Anyway, they couldn't have that after everything I had seen that night and all that I knew about them. So, they planned to kill me. Now, this 'grass rumour' wasn't true but I do know how it came about… I had previously been arrested years before for something minor, when the tape recorder was turned off the police said to me, "We know that you know Sean. If you put him in the right place at the right time then we can get you off with this."

Now I point blank refused and the coppers did not like this at all and so they set it up for this tool merchant to hopefully stab me or something so as to have just one less scumbag for them to deal with I suppose. They told Sean when they finally caught him that I had made allegations against him but later retracted them at the last minute. BULLSHIT! I had never been a 'grass' but was a long time thought of as one because of the crimes I was committing and getting away with, even after court cases which enticed people into thinking that I was trading information for a lighter punishment or even none at all. This was not the case. And I can swear this on my boy's life!!!

So, for a short while around about the same time, I was involved with a young girl, a pretty young thing but a raging coke head even her mum used to supply her every day as she was a dealer herself. To this day, I still don't know what this next geezer's problem was, all I know is it was something to do with this young girl (Chlio) and her mum, but anyway, I'm driving down Cranes Farm Road in Basildon with my mate 'Blaze' in the car with me.

Anyway, I'm driving and my phone rings, so I answer it and it's some geezer getting lemon down the phone saying he's going to stab me and kill me, and that he's one of the top boys from around the area and he's this, and he's that, I didn't really give a fuck mate, *You will bleed like anyone would so fucking try it. Oh, and he's behind me in a white BMW.* (what is it about white BMWs? huh?)

This bloke is going fucking mental down the phone (proper telephone tough guy) so I said to 'Blaze', "Listen bruv, you are gonna have to keep your mouth shut about what is about to happen!"

He said, "Why, what's going on?"

We were coming past the industrial site where B&Q is, so I pulled in there with a plan. I told 'Blaze' as the fella was following us, I was going to cut his fucking arm that he was holding his phone with, clean off and I meant it. The white BMW pulled in behind me. I pulled up right at the automatic doors/entrance, not even in a parking space and I ran into B&Q. I bought a Wilkinson sword with a 15' inch blade with like shark teeth on it for hacking through thick bushes/growth. It was fucking dangerous and scary looking and would easily shred the skin or take off a limb even with a few swings. I came out and looked at the BMW and laughed as I said, "Follow me you fucking muggy little cunt and see what happens, on my life!"

So I jumped back into my motor and said to 'Blaze', "Look bruv, I'm fucking serious I am gonna carve him up in the car park over the road!"

So I put my foot down and the white motor followed. I psyched myself up on the three-minute drive. I had to drive all the way down the road to the roundabout to turn around and head for the deserted car park behind what used to be Gloucester Park, and he was still following. It's on! This geezer hasn't got a fucking clue what he is about to get in to. I approached the car park and put my left indicator on real early to let him know I was pulling in and to follow, so I pulled in hanging out of my window and gesturing for him to follow me into the car park, and as I did, the bloke shit out and drove straight past. Like I said, 'telephone tough guy'. Fucking dick head!

The tool didn't go to waste though it helped out a few times to retrieve money I was owed and get back money for other people that were owed etc. A few weeks later, I was on foot walking to Laindon train station to meet someone for a rock (crack) and I spotted the white BMW at the red traffic lights. So I ran over to it, opened the door and pulled the geezer out and stamped on him repeatedly in the road in front of everybody and then I ran, as it was right outside Laindon police station but I think I proved my point. As long as it was the right bloke, I only went on what the car looked like. It had been modified so I'm sure it was him, huh, fucking plum! I heard no more about it!

So, I had been clean from heroin completely and everybody was hearing about me having the implants to keep me clean but what nobody knew was I was still on the crack, a hell of a lot. I'm talking thousands of pounds in a matter of hours and then meet up with my bird and try and act normal, huh, stupid boy! I had been clean from heroin for about six months and all of a sudden Carisa got in touch asking if she could come to the flat to talk as we were now both clean.

I said, "Yes, not a problem."

She started coming round and staying for a few days at a time and we started sleeping together again. This went on for about a month before Carisa would ask me a question that would change my life and scar me for forever more! She called me and said, "Is it ok if I bring a mate round to your flat? Her name's Hannah."

I said, "Yeah, no problem." This was a big mistake I was about to make when I wasn't correct in the head but didn't know it then. Half an hour later, Carisa and Hannah pulled up in a two-seater convertible Honda, (Hannah's car,) so they buzzed up to my flat and I let them in. Now apparently whilst being on heroin, I had had a big fall out and a massive row in the street outside Carisa's home with this Hannah woman but I had no recollection of it, so I didn't know what to expect.

They came in and sat down and straight away Hannah was looking around my lovely decorated flat and seeing how healthy I looked and telling me how well I had done to get off the drugs, change my life and completely turn things around (which I hadn't completely yet). Hannah was a very attractive woman, I was so attracted to her and straight away I could feel that she felt the same. A few more visits passed, Carisa turning up with Hannah, and the more this 'friend' came round the more sexual tension was building, I could feel it and I knew she could too.

One evening, I get a phone call from a private number (which I would normally ignore) but I answered it and it was Hannah saying she had my number from Carisa using her phone to call me and so she saved it on the sly. We spoke for about an hour on the phone just general chit chat and at the end of the conversation she said to me, "You deserve so much better than Carisa, you're so fit and you have done so well to come through the other side of what you have been through you must be made of some really tough stuff Scott!"

I told her to come and see me right away because I knew where she was going with this. She couldn't come right away but she said she would come alone on her lunch break the next day. I could not believe she was willing to go behind her 'best mate's back. I wondered if it was a honey trap but I thought,

Fuck it, even if it is, I don't care about losing Carisa. I'll just get a next girl. But this was no setup!

Hannah came round the next day on her lunch break at one o'clock and we chatted and listened to some music. We got on really well and had a real laugh together. She was being very flirtatious towards me and using a lot of euphemisms for sex. She was so funny and beautiful inside and out (or so I thought) as she was leaving she said, "Do you want a feel? They are real!"

She was talking about her breasts obviously. So I did (they were 36ee); they were huge, the biggest I've ever handled that's for sure. I buried my face in her chest at my front door as she was leaving and we slammed the door back shut and started to kiss passionately up against it with me lifting her off of the floor, dry humping her up against the front door. Hannah continued to visit at the same time every day for a while before I had to tell Carisa it was over and I was with her best mate. I can be a cold heartless bastard as you have probably worked out by now so I didn't care at all. Me and Hannah were officially together, BUT, she was insistent that her family did not find out until she was ready to tell them as she had been told to stay away from me as I was dangerous and I was a complete nasty bastard. She said it would be a massive kick-off when her dad finds out as he had told Hannah that if she ever went anywhere near me, he would turn his back on her forever so we kept it a secret from everyone apart from one of my mate (Ben). We would meet at his flat in the evenings so no one could catch us at mine. Hannah was telling me she wanted a baby and to get married to me despite what her family thought, huh yeah right. She was also telling me how she had no female friends and that all her mates were blokes (great! I had heard that one a million times before and it always spelt trouble).

I was so in love with this woman (already) who had just walked into my life out of nowhere, so after about a month of being together we started trying for a baby and after about two weeks she had fallen. I thought, *Yeah, this is meant to be*! As soon as we found out she was pregnant, I went straight to the bank for a loan so that I could propose to her and make it all official and done properly for us both, but especially and more so for Hannah. She was my world already. I used to call her 'angel face'. I remembered Hannah telling me how she had always dreamt of being proposed to and so I logged it in my brain and I pulled out all the stops I possibly could to make it so. I filled my flat/bedsit with about 50 lit candles and I threw red and white rose petals all over the bed and floor. I also ran a trail of rose petals from the bottom floor of the entrance to my flats all the way up the stairs to my front door and they continued throughout, they was not cheap. I had gotten a loan for the ring so that it was a nice one and not some old cheap shit. It was a stunning ring though only one carat if I remember correctly. I had Phil Collins playing on the stereo as she knocked at the door baffled by all the red and white petals leading to my door.

I said, "Come in."

As Hannah approached my living room area, I gently turned her around as she put her bag down. I took her left hand and went down on one knee and asked her if she would make me the luckiest man alive by marrying me. There was no hesitation. She said, "Yes, yes, yes," as she jumped up and down with tears in her eyes, filled with happiness and excitement. Or so it seemed! But would it last? Would it be a

191

happy ending? Would one of us fuck it up? Or would we BOTH fuck it up? Hannah told me although everything was great between us it all (the pregnancy and the engagement) had to be kept a secret from everyone so that her family didn't find out, and she was a very curvy girl and carried a little bit of weight and so could hide it for longer than, say, a skinny girl. She was 25 years old, for fuck's sake! Surely she was old enough to make her own decisions and stand by her own mistakes as in her choice of men, IF I was "A MISTAKE"!

Anyway, I said I would go along with it as long as she told them soon as I didn't want to be someone's dirty little secret but Hannah's reasons for wanting to keep it quiet went much deeper than just her family finding out. I just didn't know it. At least not for a while. Things were good for a couple of months and Hannah practically lived with me apart from the nights she 'had to stay at home' (yeah right). Every time she would turn up at mine I would notice she didn't have her ring on. I would question this and the answer was always the same, "Oh I've been around my mum and dad's and so I had to take it off, sorry."

I didn't like it and it did use to cause major arguments between us but I just had to accept it and wait for the day sometime soon that she would tell everyone and we could just be happy and really celebrate it all together as two families. I had changed. I was clean. Well, at least from the worst one (heroin) the crack was now my secret when Hannah wasn't staying but then sometimes I would have been on the crack and Hannah would call in the middle of the night asking to come over. Obviously, I said yes and had to snap out of the state I was in sharpish but I could do this simply by listening to loud music (mostly Eminem) but then as you can imagine sometimes it would send me into a dark mood. My neighbours hated me and put in numerous complaints to the council about the late-night loud music and noise. When she would come over after me being on the crack (which she had no clue about), things would often turn into an argument and in some cases, violence from both of us as I thought she was cheating on me and jumping straight out of one bed and into another. Was I right? Or was I just paranoid? One way or another I would find the truth by installing fear into Hannah and anybody that knew her. This girl is a good liar though, but I'm sure I'm right, Just a gut feeling I had.

A little while passed and I was still sure she was cheating on me with someone. Though the shock was still to come. She was just about starting to show and she told me she had told her parents who went mad apparently and they wanted nothing to do with me or the baby, huh convenient. I was at work one day with Colin 'my stepdad' and I got a phone call from a friend who starts by saying, "Fisher, where are you bruv?"

I said, "At work mate. Why, what's up?"

He said to me, "Look mate, I don't know how to put this so please stay calm. I am in Mothercare on the A127 and I am about fifth in the queue. Your missus is being served and she's just done over £300 pound on baby stuff!"

I said, "Yeah, so what's the problem?"

He said, "Err some geezer has just paid for it all bruv, she's with him."

I said, "okay, thanks mate. Don't get seen and leave it with me!"

Now I had to think. Then my mobile rings and its Hannah.

She said, "Hi babe, my mate Tereasa has just bought us a few bits for the baby."

I said, "Oh sweet, put her on so I can say thanks."

She told me the 'mate' wasn't with her, she had gone into another shop, again bloody convenient. Now I knew something was going on, I just had to find out what so I could deal with it in any way I saw fit. Normally serious violence to the fella would be my answer to this. I sat on it for a while and didn't say a word to Hannah until I knew exactly what was what. Not a good idea because then when I blow, I blow bigtime having held it in. In the meantime, I hear Hannah has been seen with a fella named Tommy. Now, I knew Tommy very well and Hannah didn't know that, so I called him and asked what the fuck was going on. He was a nice bloke Tom, good looking and a real nice bloke. He informed me that he had been seeing Hannah for a few weeks but had messed about with her for months and she had been telling him the baby was his. So now I know she's cheating. I explained to Tommy that we were engaged to be married and the baby was planned, he was shocked and could not apologise enough to me but like I told him he was not the one cheating on me, she was. He called it off with her obviously and she still has no idea I know anything at this time. Then I hear she is seeing her ex fella too. I get a phone call one day, it goes like this, "Fisher, your bird is in the five bells car park in a flash motor with some ugly bloke with a ponytail!"

Again I simply said, "Leave it with me and thanks."

I went straight to the car park with a friend who I won't name as he is still an active criminal and in and out of prison. Anyway, he always had guns around him, so we went together in my car and as soon as I pulled in I see them sitting there in the corner by the bushes, who knows what they were about to get up to (I knew how filthy Hannah was sexually). I stepped out of the car and fired a shot (from a little 2.2') at the car after screaming at them, "Fucking look out you cunts!"

I missed all together thankfully as I could have been banged up for it if I had hit one of them (put in prison) then they would all of beaten me and above all the innocent baby could have been harmed. I didn't consider this though as I was in fucking pieces over all this cheating bollocks. I would never have cheated on her and so did not expect it in return. It's not like she needed the sex elsewhere as we were at it all the time for days at a time even. It was great.

One night, it was new year's eve and Hannah told me she had a family party that her dad had organised and obviously I would not be welcome or even invited. Hannah said that she 'had to be there for the family', so we wouldn't be spending new year's together. Shit!!! Anyway, I think I got cracked up to the point that I didn't even acknowledge when it struck 12 o'clock. I was on another planet after spending the evening indoors with three mates all on the 'pipe' (crack). Once everyone had left at about 2 o'clock in the morning, my mood changed dramatically and I became paranoid to the point that I was hiding on my little balcony ducked down outside so no one could see me in the cold. I was in and out of my flat like a fiddlers elbow not knowing what to do with myself. After about half an hour of me freaking out all alone, Hannah called and said she was two minutes away and she wanted to stay the night. I was over the moon. When she walked in, I clocked that she didn't have our engagement ring on which instantly pissed me off and added to my paranoia as to where she had REALLY been? She strolled in as cool as you like and took her jacket off and straight away started to undress. I thought, *Yes, my new year's luck just changed!* and she was good! But completely out of character for her, she wanted to climb into bed and go straight to sleep. As I said this was well out of the ordinary for her, something was amiss here. If I got a thought in my head, I was fucking dangerous, especially if it involved someone else fucking my girl. I climbed into bed and Hannah wasn't even facing me she was facing the wall. What? Weird!

So, I got up close to her and started to kiss the back of her neck. She turned around and went to kiss me back and as she did I got a strong smell of cum (semen) on her breath as if she had been sucking someone's dick. I knew this smell VERY, VERY, well from my childhood due to something that happened to me! (something that was to come out much later in life). I instantly flipped out and I jumped out of the bed as quick as I had ever moved before, and I dragged Hannah out of the bed with me by her hair. She was kicking and trying to punch me and screaming at the top of her voice, "Help me, he's going to kill me!" but the neighbours were used to all the commotion and drama and screaming and so nobody was called, like the police thankfully because I was like a wild fucking animal and they would have banged me up for sure as I would probably have attacked them too what with the mood I was in. A lot of the rest of the night was a blur partly because of the massive amount of crack I had smoked but also the red mist had descended down on me but to me, it's more like a blackout that I forget all about within seconds of it happening and it can last for hours or even days. Me and Hannah struggled on the floor for a second before I got control of her and I picked her up and threw her on to the sofa and as I did, I jumped on top of her. As I jumped, she put her arm up to stop me landing on her and as I landed on her arm she screamed. This was a blood-curdling scream this time. She was clearly in serious agony, something bad had happened, even I sobered up instantly and came back around 'sort of'. I wondered if she putting it on to stop me but no one I had ever met can act that well. I could see she was in a lot of pain and needed medical attention asap as she was clutching her left arm in floods of tears. We had both been drinking all night and so I had to call an ambulance. I don't remember how long we waited for it but I do remember being down on my knees at her side whilst begging her for forgiveness for hours and asking her if she was going to report me to the police. Her arm was clearly broken so when the ambulance arrived we got in and went to A&E to wait for five hours to be seen. I did ask, and Hannah wanted me with her despite what had happened, I was shocked she hadn't told me to fuck off. Whilst we were waiting, Hannah said, "Let's go and have a 'quicky' in the disabled toilets."

So I immediately agreed and off we went one at a time so no one noticed and we did the deed in Basildon hospital disabled toilets! Hmm, classy I know! Now that she had done that I felt everything was okay again. I was sitting with my girl with a broken arm THAT I DID. Disgusting. I still feel ashamed to this day. After x-rays confirmed Hannah's arm was broke in two (a clean break), she was quizzed by doctors about domestic violence/abuse and Hannah denied it all the way to protect me for some strange reason (bless her). Perhaps she did love me in some weird way. We left the hospital once the cast had been put on and I had to beg and beg Hannah to come back with me. She wanted to go to her dad's where she lived when she wasn't at mine and tell them that she had got drunk and had a fall, but I thought that if she went I would never see her again so like I said, I begged and she came back with me but she was real quiet and different for obvious reasons which in turn made me feel on edge, it was a vicious circle. This time I had gone too far. We had had fights before but the outcome was never like this. I was surprised that she agreed to come back with me; I think it was out of fear sadly. It wasn't long after this the truth all really came out.

One night, I had been told that day by a friend that knew her, that my girl had been chatting all day to her ex on the phone. Now I thought Hannah still had a hang-up about her ex as he had the ponytail and she liked long hair on a man and I know that when she was with him he refused to have kids with her so what did she do? She sucked his cock until he'd cum in her mouth and she'd walk into the bathroom whilst holding the semen in her mouth and she spat it into a syringe and shot it up inside herself to try and get pregnant 'by mistake' with him and trap him. She told 'a close friend' this but what she didn't realise was most of the girls she knew fancied me and told me all the gossip. I knew it all. Ha. Got to stay one step ahead in life! Or at least try to.

One night I could take no more, I wanted proof and to catch her red-handed. So I thought, *Right, I need to get hold of her phone and check the history on it, like calls and texts*, as there was no internet at the time that I remember, certainly not on mobile phones anyway. So, when Hannah finished work and had apparently been having dinner at her parent's house and came to mine after, I was in a paranoid state and feeling angry and upset. I now knew she was cheating, so when she got to mine I said, "Give me your phone Hannah."

She said, "No, what for?"

Straight away my alarm bells rang in my head. 'What is she hiding?' I attacked her and instantly flew off the handle in a rage and she managed to lock herself on my balcony to my flat and made a call to my mum saying I was losing it again and could she help? My mum left her house right away and arrived at mine within ten minutes. Whilst Hannah was calling my mum for help, I was calling my best mate Ross, he got on a BMX bike with no gear's on it and rode a 30-minute ride in 15 minutes and he was there to try and calm the situation. It was blurred for a while as usual but I remember when my mum and Ross were there, I asked again for Hannah's phone again she refused. So I ran at her with my mum and Ross trying to stop me from killing her. I grabbed the handle of her handbag and everyone was holding onto it. All three of them. I pulled so hard all three of them fell forward onto the floor and I got the bag containing the mobile phone I was after. I looked through it and Hannah had been on the phone to her ex all day on and off when I couldn't get a hold of her. I started to lose the fucking plot and I grabbed a knife and grabbed Hannah by the hair to cut her throat for lying to me. My mum intervened once again and said, "Look Scott, please calm down, you will have to stab me first. Look let's call him and find out what's going on!"

so I said, "Yeah, go for it please."

So my mum called the fella and he said Hannah had been seeing him for a few weeks whilst being engaged to me but he knew nothing of the engagement. And she had told him that she was scared because she had, had a "one-night stand" with Scott Fisher (me) and she thought she had fallen pregnant by this 'one-off'. My mum said, "No mate, they are engaged and have been trying for a baby."

He was shocked as were we all. I was gutted and didn't know how to take it or how to deal with it. After everyone sitting us down and making us talk, Hannah ended up staying again. Things were weird between us but Hannah seemed to be spending more time and nights with me. After about a week, Hannah woke up one morning as normal, I was just stirring and she said to me, "Babe, do you need anything from the town?" I said, "Yeah, grab me a lynx deodorant and some toothpaste please 'Angel Face'," and off she went to the town six months pregnant. We were getting on well and I couldn't wait for her to get back. Only thing was I would be waiting a long time as that morning was the last time I would ever see Hannah EVER. Her parents put her into hiding somewhere so I couldn't find her. I never saw her again! Or the baby girl! This would seriously fuck my head up as I was so, so desperate for a baby. I believed it would have been the making of me. This would be half the reason I would go away for seven years. Oh, and yeah, it turned out she was sleeping with four of us fellas and telling us all that the baby was ours. So, all four of us were buying things for what we thought was our baby. Who knows who the father is really. Not nice to put it mildly. Fucking NEXT!!!!

You have to be a heartless bastard of some sorts to deal with something like this and not top yourself or kill someone else, especially being me!

Before I left, I must say, one of the biggest helping hands I had to stay away from the heroin was MUSIC…

When I was young and on the pills etc, I was into my garage music but was never an 'MC' or anything and had never thought of even trying although I did use to mimic people like MC Neat and Creed just as a laugh but when I got clean from heroin, I fell into rap and hip hop in a massive way. It almost became the light at the end of the tunnel 'the answer to everything'. Going back a bit, the first rapper I listened to was Eminem. A friend of mine bought a cassette tape back from a holiday to America when I was 17 years old of Eminem and I was amazed straight away with the sheer talent and comedy value to his early stuff but later in life (when I hit 20 years old), this rapper (with his darker stuff) would get me through the darkest times of my life. Or at least one of the most difficult time for sure. I loved everything about this fella and still do. In my eyes, he's an absolute genius. I would become likened by many people to this genius/legend by some big people in the music industry, who I can't name as I do not have permission. So how would I get this reputation having never rapped before? Well, it all started when I stopped the heroin but I was still having late night £800 sessions on the crack to myself and just listening to Eminem all night long. After a while, I started to write lyrics myself and found myself writing things that when I read them back over an Eminem track in time to the beat, I felt like I was sounding pretty good. There were times I amazed myself with my own words as I just didn't know where they were coming from or how I was rhyming them.

I found out I was good when I bumped into an old friend named Ben. Now, I hadn't seen Ben since I was on the heroin and we had a big fall out and I had someone (a friend named Tommy Broomfield) give him a little warning for me as he was going around saying, "he was going to clump me when he sees me." Tommy Broomfield didn't take to kindly to this and so with his cousins, they attacked Ben and his four mates at Craylands shops. It was all over the fact that I had knocked

Ben's dad (he used to buy power tools from us as kids). I think I owed him £80 if my memory serves me right and I never paid and so the relationship between me and Ben was not good anymore, but I was clean now and had changed dramatically. I see Ben in his car outside my flat years later and I flagged him down to stop. He pulled over as he was always up for a row, he said, "What the fuck do you want?"

I said to him, "Look bruv, I miss ya! I know I owe your dad money and I'm happy to give it to you right now mate! How much is it?"

He told me and I pulled it out there and then and paid him. Anyway, back to the rapping. Me and Ben went back to my flat and he informed me he had just moved in two roads down from me. He asked me what I had been up to and how was I doing staying away from the smack. I told him music was helping me and I had started to write rap lyrics myself. Ben just laughed as I had never been known to do anything like this and didn't exactly look 'the rapper' type but he said, "okay, let's hear ya then."

So I wacked on the Nelly and Kelly's 'dilemma' instrumental I had managed to get hold of, and I rapped for the first time ever in front of someone and I was anxious to see if he was going to take the piss out of me as Ben is not one to hold back with his thoughts or words and will let you know how it is. He said that he could not believe it and he never for a minute expected what came out of my mouth. He was repeatedly asking me if I had really written it myself and I had to convince him that I had and it was completely original. Like I said, this is one fella that if he thought I was shit he would have said there and then and made a big joke of it but he was honestly stunned and speechless for a while when I finished 'spitting'. The first set of lyrics I ever wrote read…

Man, I can't believe after all this time,
All this thinking of this girl and how she'd never be mine,
I was always thinking of a way that I could make her my own,
Take her away and keep her and share a 10 bedroom home,
And even if it was away from everybody that I knew,
I really couldn't give a fuck as long as our love grew,
But into something much stronger than the one I had before,
Coz You know I don't need to be seeing no replica whore,
Or even a girl that REMINDS me of the one I had last,
I'll end up chocking ya motherfucking filthy arse,
Especially if ya take advantage in the way that she did,
But take advantage like an angel then my love'll fall deep,
But Then you know that I've fell for you forever and a day,
Didn't I tell you the day would come when I would get my way,
And you'd be ready to say 'I do' to me all the way,
Down the aisle, while ya man's still fucking back in the day,
He's loving his own way and he's thinking that he's fine,
But I've taken his best ever girl and I've made her mine,
And if he couldn't even see how much this woman was worth,
This motherfucker must have been a blind beggar from birth,

But then I thought he was a beggar from the way he went on,

And the way he kept telling his girl he was the don,

And he could never live up to it so then she moved on,

That's why she came to me coz I could see she was the bomb,

Now I'm gonna keep this girl forevermore by my side,

Coz I know how to feel her, take her out n' treat her right,

And if the next man approaches from behind wannin a fight,

I know I can turn my back and let my girl finish the night,

I know I wouldn't have to do what I would normally do,

Grab this fool around the neck and make it clear 'she ain't with you',

I know shell do it herself, coz she's my number two,

Now it's only her I have to remind that this is true,

She's only my number two because I'm my own number one,

And I only keep it that way to keep us up and with the fun,

I only keep it the same to keep you up and on the run,

I only EVER keep ya going,

Only to keep ya knowing…that…

No, I ain't never ever gonna go anywhere… WE could never, ever share anything we like,

Right there…with no cares…and no one ever around us to interfere…

I was there for you when you first ran,

That's why ya came running to me instead of running to ya own man,

Girl I was your confidant…

But all along that was just a plan to make sure that I was the man that won,

And make sure you came to me, coz I could see ya man weren't never gonna give ya everything ya need,

girl I think you know you need to give him up, up, and come and be with me n' my other girl, they call her lady luck, fuck,

we'll be making sure that you're luck's changed, making sure that this time around it don't feel the same, something ya man can't and won't never do shit, coz your man's not a superstar...

ya mans a dick, he'll never be able to make you feel how I make you feel, when I show bout my love, and how it's so fucking real,

I'd put that...ring on ya finger girl,

Take you all around the world,

Bring you back...marry you and turn you into my girl!!!

That was the first two verses I ever wrote and Ben was amazed by this. He said to me that he knew a music producer who would be able to make me my own beats probably for just a small fee. So I asked him to find the bloke. Anyway, months passed and there was no joy finding this music producer named 'Darren Munt'. As the time passed and there was no contact with this bloke, I started to lose hope and then one day Ben was walking through Basildon when he saw someone under his bonnet obviously broke down so Ben approached the fella to ask if he needed help. The bloke turned around and it was Darren Munt. It was like it was meant to happen as Darren didn't even live in Basildon anymore and he lived in London, so the chances of this happening were slim to none. Ben took his number and called me to let me know straight away. I didn't really know what to expect so I can't say I was excited by it at all but it was something to do to keep me away from heroin, and IT WORKS!!! At least temporarily, if not forever. Would I stay clean through music?

Before me and Darren met, I went to a studio on Cranes Farm Road in Basildon armed with a CD of hip hop instrumentals and I recorded my own lyrics that I had written, over them. I took a friend with me and while I was recording, I took a break and went down to the toilets to 'powder my nose'. I had a wrap of cocaine on me so I went to have a sniff and then when I returned, he was all excited and said he had to talk to me. He told me that he had overheard the two fellas that were recording me saying that I was going to make them an absolute fortune and that I was a major talent. But I made my mixtape and I never heard a thing from them so I guess they were full of shit! A lot of people in the music industry are, unfortunately, and I have met quite a few of them along the way but would I ever make it big up against these idiots?

After making the dodgy mixtape, I finally had Darren Munt's number to contact him. So I wasted no time and I called him to chat about the type of music he was used to making to see if I thought I could work with him. He told me he was into garage (old school) and now hip hop and rap. Wow, this could be a match made in heaven. I couldn't wait to meet him, he sounded well clued up, and from what he had been told by Ben, he was really excited at the thought of working alongside/collaborating with me. This was fast becoming a passion as opposed to just a hobby and I was aiming for the skies. I not only wanted to be as big as Eminem but I was being told that I was on par with him, especially when I started I rapped with an American accent as that was all I knew. There was no UK hip hop scene really at all and no grime that I had ever heard apart from So Solid Crew and there was no such thing as 'Drill' music. Not like now. So, me and Darren arranged to meet. He would pick me up from my flat in Laindon and take me to the three bedroom house he shared with two other music students all using their rooms as fully kitted out, soundproof studios. These boys eat, sleep and shit music; it's all they knew. They were all three in Thames valley university studying and producing music. So Darren came to get me and the girl I was with at the time named Hayley. He picked us up and drove to the studio/house in south Ealing where he lived. When we got there, I bought myself four cans of Stella Artois and rolled myself a fat skunk joint. Darren looked at me as if to say 'you ain't recording shit after all that mate' but he was in for a bit of a shock and I think to this day he would still agree.

When we spoke on the phone Darren asked me for some sort of idea for a tune, ya know 'what would I like?' So I came up with the idea of using a sample of the godfather film theme tune over a hip hop beat. Darren loved the idea and so he ran with it and had it sort of ready when I got there. So I listened to the beat I think three times and then I said, "okay, I'm ready, I love it, let's do this!"

So I put on the headphones and jumped in front of the mic with the popper stopper a cm away from my lips. I felt like I had made it already. Fuck the money, I was buzzing, but was that just the beer and the joint I had smoked? I was doing something that was giving me a natural buzz. Something I had been pursuing with hard drugs for years only this was not bad for my health. Wow, I was in heaven. I want to do this forever! After we had recorded the track, me and Darren together were a work of art, and we both knew it. Darren came up with the idea that he would use me for his end of term project at university, this way we would both be gaining and he could work with me for a lower sum of money for each track and his time, as it was to benefit him too as he thought I was so good and easy to work with and I would make him look good too. I can record a track 'in one take' with no autotune and 'track it' in one too and this makes the producers job a damn site easier.

After the first time of visiting Darren in the studio, I came up with an idea. I thought I could rip off an Eminem track just close enough to sound like it but not enough to infringe on the copyright. Darren asked why I wanted to do this, my reply was simple. I said, "Look Darren, if I make this clever enough and I can get it heard in the right places, Eminem or his people will get to hear it. Now we know that if someone runs Eminem down, he retaliates normally, now if I can get him to hit back at me, I have made it and cheated my way in."

Darren was all over it, he thought it sounded brilliant so that's what we did. We ripped off the tune 'Just lose it', it was all basically a comedy/commercial track calling Eminem gay along with Dr Dre and a few others. (you can find this on YouTube under, Anjal-just lost it (Eminem spoof). We worked on this and got it done in a day along with two other tracks but that was the one that had to be perfect. So over the next few months, me and Darren built a portfolio for his university work (his final project). One day we were recording, I was on the mic and Darren was at the pc, half-way through he stopped the track and I didn't know why because I was on fire. He turned to me and said, "Bruv, you are a fucking GENIUS! Unbelievable mate!!"

Coming from someone that really knows their stuff this meant a lot. I was buzzing hard just on life and music alone (oh, and the joints again). So, months passed and we worked together a lot and made a 12 track album including skits, comedy tracks and darker stuff too. Darren was so excited about the results he was going to get for this project on me, we even recorded a video to accompany the Eminem diss track but to be honest, a load of people dropped out including the makeup artist all on the morning. There were a lot of things that went wrong on the day and to be honest I don't even own a copy of the DVD as it was a fucking shambles and quite embarrassing to watch. I could have produced it better myself on the streets and really wish I had!

Anyway, just after a year, Darren was finished with his project on me and he was real proud of it and so was I. I really thought it would stir controversy in the industry and get us in. Darren said, "What if Shady Records sues us?"

I said, "What the fuck for? We ain't got nothing mate! Let em do it! It's our names in the paper! Overnight publicity and instant fame Darren! Fuck it bruv."

So before trying to release it independently Darren surrendered it to his professors at university, he was pulled aside in the lesson and told in no uncertain circumstances could he ever release that track. Because if he did Eminem's people would take him for everything and end his music career permanently and he would never make music again. Now I understood that he pulled the plug and wouldn't let me release the track as he owned the copyright to the beat and I did for the lyrics, but I still wanted to go ahead as this tune was so, so, clever, and I believed that if Marshall Mathers had heard it he would have heard pure talent very much like his own. We were so close I could almost taste the fame, I really thought we were going to make it. The girl I was taking with me was star-struck simply because a producer (a good one) was calling me 'a genius' and I was smashing out three tracks a day easily, like I said I can do three verses in one take with no problems and 'track' them too. There were times I would turn up at Darren's without even ever hearing the tunes beforehand and I would get there and write a track to the beat in the space of ten minutes. Again, Darren would be amazed. I don't know if that was just a tactic to push me and spur me on to be better but if it was, it worked, because he made me feel like I was going to be big in the game and we were going to go all the way. I was still in the frame of mind that I wanted to put the tune out and just take the backlash off of it. At least my name would be out there in the same breath as Eminem, and in my eyes, that cannot be a bad thing. I recorded with Darren for years even when I hit 25 years old and I was living abroad. I still flew over monthly to record in the studio. I loved it and even though I wasn't making any money, I felt like a superstar. I was living the dream as far as I was concerned. All I was missing was performing live but there were times me and Darren would finish recording for the day, generally early as we worked so quick together, and we would go out and find a pub with live music of some sort as we were both into all sorts of genres of music and could appreciate pretty much anything live, but every time after having a good drink in a pub, we would leave and almost always bump into a crowd of black lads all rapping at each other in a circle taking turns. The first time we spotted a group Darren said, "Get in there son, show em what you got."

I didn't need to think twice, I approached the group and waited for whoever was rapping at the time to stop then I would come out with something like...

You better run motherfucker,

I'm a young gun bucker,

Chucking lyrics at each other,

I'm a hip hop fuck up,

And I can't find no other way for me to find a place,

In this shamed disgraced game that you seem to call a race,

But let's face it,

The race is basic,

And it's only the faces that you know up in the game that makes it,

I ain't wasted yet, I'm gonna make my tape, shit,

And put it out myself for all you fuckers to taste it,

Coz I'm finally brazen, it's amazing.

I couldn't give a fuck about anybody's aching.

I'm making...the most of what I've got and I'm taking,

The jackpot, right up to the top,

Am I faking?

I hope not,

I'm shaking and am I on the verge of breaking,

Am I quaking, the bottom of my legs are aching,

Am I faking, yeah ya know you could be right,

I ain't aching so fuck it, let's fight tonight,

It's five to nine little prick time to die,

I got another five minutes I got my nine to five,

I got nine lives bitch n' now it's time to ride,

My life of crimes yelling for the time of nine,

It's like a bullet in line saves time,

But then again a stitch in time could save your life,

Fuck it bruv, I put a bullet in ya side, one in each of your eyes.

Motherfucker, now its hindsight,

And I'm bright,

Tight when I rhyme in the limelight,

Motherfucker n' I rhyme tight,

Let me shed a little light upon the situation, alright,

Now the race is on so hold tight...

I can pronunciate,

And I can calculate,

and I can tell if you will an even shall be late,

I shall be great,

With a fresh shallow grave,

Dug for you for when ya standing in the shower brave,

And then ya power fades

And then an hour gains,

And I'm looking at ya face n' I'm ahead of the games

(But the game just ain't the same,)

(It's changing, it's a new game,)

Then you better start playing,

In case the game changes again,

When somebody gets fame,

Somebody VOWELS they're not playing,

Man, look now there's so many rows the games changed,

Again the point one to me the who... An...jal,

A quick look back motherfucker what now,

A kid took that big bad boy crown,

Ya big bad boy got a big bad frown,

Big bad boy left ya big bad town,

Motherfucker it's time for you to wanna step down,

Save face, say grace, say respect to the crowd,

Say what you want but when ya done jump down,

Motherfucker ya times up n' I'm up now!!!!

And really, I could go on, it was second nature to me somehow. Writing is the best therapy I have ever found and I have been on ecstasy, speed, crack, heroin, cocaine, ketamine, weed and prescription drugs all my life. Yet when I rap to a crowd anywhere, whether it be in a pub on karaoke or in a crowd on the street, I've always had a real good reception. I buzz so hard, it's such a high, and at the same time, nothing was going to stop me and my producer. Apart from…a WOMAN!!!

Yeah, that's right. I call Darren from abroad to come over and record. I hadn't spoken to him in two months or so (which was long for us). Anyway, in this time Darren has sold up the studio, given up the music and moved in with a bird. I was devastated, to say the least. I met up with a few foreign producers after this, in the country I was in, but we were just not on the same page at all. Me and Darren clicked and was smashing it but now I had lost my producer. I gave up on the music though I still love it with a passion and listen to music every day of my life. It gets me through the toughest of times. I lose myself in music completely and can do that for hours and hours. Even days. I still write lyrics but have no producer so it's literally just therapy. I still have the poor man's copyright on 12 sets of lyrics and I have loads that are more recent and up with the times on paper and in my head, but I miss pressing my lips on the popper stopper in front of the mic. I feel alive when I'm doing that. I have been offered to go on pirate stations time and time again and I have just blown it out. I have never heard of anyone making it big from pirate stations apart from DJ Luck and MC Neat, and that was in 1999/2000 fucking 17 years ago and good luck to them they are still going strong but there is no room for anyone else on that scene, at least while they are still about. At least that's how it seems. Plus, obviously, I am a rapper, not an MC but even the rap scene in this country is dead (though it is growing) there are about four artists I hear of on a regular basis. It's just a shame I was never in the right place at the right time because without blowing my own trumpet, I am more than good.

When Darren gave up, I gave up, and that was the end of that. What a Shame!!

If there were a few rules I lived by, they were, I never got greedy and I quit while I was ahead. Also, I KEPT MY MOUTH SHUT! I just didn't say anything, to anybody without thinking first, but that's how I got away with the lot. Don't take that as a tip, take it as a warning. I look over my shoulder to this very day!!!

So...after all the drama, at 20 years old I decided to go away, now it's time to fuck up and get into trouble somewhere in another country for a while I guess. Don't worry when I get the chance, I'll send you all another 80,000 word 'postcard' on how it went.

As Vinnie Jones said in *Lock, Stock...* "It's been emotional!"

Peace!!!

Epilogue

Well… after all that, where did I end up?

As this story is released, I am 39 years old, I am back in England.

After living abroad for seven years, on my return I entered into a mentally abusive, coercive and controlling relationship, this went on for ten years. I finally managed to gather the courage and strength to get out of it just over a year ago. I took my five-year-old son from this terrible relationship with me and I walked out! This is thanks to the fact that I have met a woman who I knew as a kid (13 years old), Her name is Chloe and she has been my absolute saviour! Since I met up with her again in February 2020 she has given me the strength to not just walk away from the mental torture and abuse I was suffering at the hands of another woman, but to take my son, take the whole thing to court, represent myself in court and go on to win custody of my son from Monday to Friday every week with visitation with his mother at the weekends. In the last year Chloe and I have merged our families together as one. We got married in the COVID lockdown in October 2020 and we are now expecting our first child together. A little girl.' Sophia Slaven: Due 29th March 2021.

I have really turned my life around in a massive way.

Yes I have had a lot of support from my family and my wonderful wife, who I cannot thank enough, but if you are not lucky enough to have a support network, there is help out there in the form of the mental health teams and drug rehabilitation centres in every area of the country.

I have also stopped ALL illicit drugs including cocaine, crack, ketamine and weed which I smoked for 27 years and I have stopped all the prescription drugs that I was addicted to and not supposed to be on, which I was when I started this story. I have now been totally clean for over a year and will be forever. I still suffer with anxiety, but my psychotic disorder is in remission and no longer effects my daily life which I believe is down to stopping all the drugs. I am no longer violent in any way to anybody. I want this story to let people know that you CAN turn your life around no matter what you are going through, even if you feel so low that you just want to give up and die, You CAN do it, just as I have! If I can do it after everything I have been through, then anybody can! Mental health teams are amazing these days and they recognize that some people need help more than others, they DO help!

Believe in yourself, YOU are your strength, you can do this!

It really doesn't matter how low you go on the wrong road you can climb back onto the right road and I am proof of this!

Do not take this story as an example, please, take it as a LESSON!

Stand up and fight.
You can do it!

Ingram Content Group UK Ltd.
Milton Keynes UK
UKHW021841240323
419126UK00004B/49

9 781528 981255